ORDER
MY STEPS
IN THY
WORD

*In recognition of the dedication of
The Word Over The World Auditorium
this book is lovingly published
with joyful thanksgiving.*

Other books by Victor Paul Wierwille

Receiving the Holy Spirit Today
Are the Dead Alive Now?
Power for Abundant Living
Studies in Abundant Living Series
  Volume I, *The Bible Tells Me So*
  Volume II, *The New, Dynamic Church*
  Volume III, *The Word's Way*
  Volume IV, *God's Magnified Word*
Jesus Christ Is Not God
Jesus Christ Our Passover
Jesus Christ Our Promised Seed

ORDER MY STEPS IN THY WORD

Volume V

Studies in Abundant Living

Victor Paul Wierwille

American Christian Press
The Way International
New Knoxville, Ohio 45871

The scriptures used throughout this book are quoted from the King James Version unless otherwise noted. All explanatory insertions by the author within a scripture verse are enclosed in brackets. All Greek and Hebrew words are printed with English letters and italicized.

International Standard Book Number 0-910068-59-3
Library of Congress Catalog Card Number 70-176281
American Christian Press
The Way International
New Knoxville, Ohio 45871
© 1985 by The Way International
All rights reserved
First Edition 1985. Third Printing 1985
Printed in the United States of America

CONTENTS

Preface   ix

Part I God's Order for Life

   1. *God Almighty—El Shaddai*   5
   2. *God's Blueprint of Creation*   21
   3. *Heirs Together of the Grace of Life*   39

Part II God's Order for Leadership

   4. *The Qualities of a Spiritual Leader*   57
   5. *The Qualifications for Ordination*   79
   6. *The Higher Powers of Romans 13*   93
   7. *The Transfer of Leadership*   107

Part III God's Order in Old Testament Times

   8. *A Man in Whom the Spirit of God Is*   141
   9. *Choose You This Day*   171
 10. *The Way of Life or Death*   187

Part IV God's Order for Quality Believers

 11. *Climbing High to Seek Truth*   207
 12. *The Mark of Quality*   223
 13. *The Light of Life*   239
 14. *Quickened Together with Christ*   253

    Scripture Index   291

    About the Author   299

PREFACE

The title of this volume, *Order My Steps in Thy Word,* comes from Psalms 119:133.

> Order my steps in thy word:
> and let not any iniquity
> have dominion over me.

It is my soul's sincere desire to have my life ordered, or established, in God's Word. His standard is the standard I want for my life. When my steps are ordered according to the standard of God's Word, no iniquity or sin can have any power over me because I'm living my life God's way. God's order and iniquity are mutually exclusive. Where God's order is, iniquity can have no dominion. And where iniquity has dominion, God's order is excluded.

God designed life—He made, formed, and created us. Therefore He certainly knows what richness of life He intended for us when we live life according to His plan. When we believers line up our lives according to God's Word, God's rule book, we put ourselves in the position to receive the maximum blessings of life—in body, soul, and spirit.

Order My Steps in Thy Word is organized into four parts: "God's Order for Life," "God's Order for Leadership," "God's Order in Old Testament Times," and "God's Order for Quality Believers." Within the parts, each chapter has been researched and written as an individual study. The studies are grouped under general topics so that you as the reader can gain a broader scope of each topic. I pray and believe that a greater knowledge of God and His Word will uplift you and inspire you to better order your steps in God's Word.

PART I

GOD'S ORDER FOR LIFE

PART I

GOD'S ORDER FOR LIFE

God Himself is order. As a matter of course then, His creation has order. God ordered the universe and everything in it. He even ordered a way of life for each individual. The three chapters which make up Part I, "God's Order for Life," demonstrate God's plan. The first chapter shows that God, Who is *Elohim* and *Jehovah,* is also *El Shaddai,* God Almighty. And when God Almighty, the God of all might, works for His children, absolutely no obstacle is insurmountable.

"God's Blueprint for Creation" describes how God so beautifully planned the interrelationships between Himself, man, the earth, and the universe.

"Heirs Together of the Grace of Life" explains God's original plan and His will for families, most specifically for the husband and wife who want to order their relationship according to God's Word.

3

When we know and understand God's order for life, and how carefully and lovingly He prepared for us and provided for our every need, our hearts overflow with wonder and thanksgiving for our loving heavenly Father.

Chapter One

GOD ALMIGHTY—*EL SHADDAI*

There are some men in this world who are willing for God to be the God of heaven, but they are not willing for Him to be the God on earth. The Lord's Prayer says, "Our Father which art in heaven, Hallowed be thy name. Thy kingdom come. Thy will be done in earth, as *it is* in heaven." Although the prayer says, "Thy will be done in earth," most people want their own wills to be done here on earth.

Man's reasoning—no matter how enlightened or how logical he may believe that he is—will never give man a true knowledge of God. Only the revelation from God in His Word does that. In order to see the greatness of our God as the "Almighty God," we must observe God's revelation of Himself.

One way God lets us know Who He is is through the titles He gives Himself. God refers to Himself by a number of different names in His Word. In verse 1 of Genesis 1, God reveals Himself by the Hebrew word *Elohim,* the

5

Creator. In the second chapter of Genesis He uses the name *Jehovah,* denoting His relationship to what He created. In this study I would like to delve into the scriptures which reveal God as *El Shaddai,* translated "God Almighty" or "Almighty God." Genesis 17:1 contains the first occurrence of this name. In Biblical research, the first use of a word or a term or an expression must be studied most carefully for its significance. What is the great truth concerning this name for God, *El Shaddai,* in its first use?

> Genesis 17:1:
> And when Abram was ninety years old and nine, the Lord appeared to Abram, and said unto him, I *am* the Almighty God [*El Shaddai*]. . . .

God didn't say to Abram, "I am *Jehovah*" or "I am *Elohim*"; He said, "I am the Almighty God," *El Shaddai* in Hebrew. *El* is "God," *Shaddai* is "almighty." He is the Almighty God. Now what does it mean that our God, Who is *Elohim* and *Jehovah,* is also *El Shaddai,* the Almighty God? What exactly is being revealed to us about God? Let's observe the rest of the verse which contains this name.

...I *am* the Almighty God [*El Shaddai*];
walk before me, and be thou perfect.

Often I pray, "Almighty God, unto whom
every heart is opened...." I do not use these
words haphazardly. Why should I? I study God's
Word so that I know what the words "Almighty
God" stand for. I want to know what they mean
Biblically, and then I endeavor to use them accurately.

"...I *am* the Almighty God; walk before me,
and be thou perfect." The text literally says
"walk before me and you are complete." "Walk
and be complete." Walk upon what? "The revelation *I* have given you. Don't walk by your reasoning or your opinions, but by the revelation
that I have given you."

Verse 2:
And I [*El Shaddai,* Almighty God] will
make my covenant between me and thee,
and [I] will multiply thee exceedingly.

God said to Abram in Canaan, "I, your
Almighty God, will make a covenant with you. I
will see to it that your offspring will be exceedingly numerous." The pronoun "I" refers

7

back to God as *El Shaddai,* Almighty God in verse 1, throughout this section of Genesis.

> Verses 3 and 4:
> And Abram fell on his face: and God talked with him [revelation], saying,
>
> As for me, behold, my covenant *is* with thee, and thou shalt be a father of many nations.

Abram's heart's desire was to have children. And so as Abram carried out God Almighty's promise of Genesis 17:1 to walk before God and be complete, Abram received the fulfillment of that promise: God would make Abram "a father of many nations."

> Verse 5:
> Neither shall thy name any more be called Abram....

The word "Abram" in Hebrew means "father of height." God wanted this man to have a more appropriate name, so He renamed him.

> ...but thy name shall be Abraham....

God gave Abram the new name "Abraham."

And the word "Abraham" means "father of a great multitude" or "father of many nations." The name "Abram" no longer accurately described God's man. God saw him as the father of a great multitude, so that's what He called him.

Now Abraham, this father of a great multitude, was a friend of God. God says in James 2:23: "And the scripture was fulfilled which saith, Abraham believed God, and it was imputed unto him for righteousness: and he was called the Friend of God." Isaiah 41:8 states, "But thou, Israel, *art* my servant, Jacob whom I have chosen, the seed of Abraham my friend." What a relationship God and Abraham had!

Genesis 17:5:
...for a father of many nations have I [*El Shaddai,* Almighty God] made thee.

"God Almighty" put in the past tense what to Abraham was still future, was yet to come to pass. The words "Almighty God" indicate that He is a God Who is an all-powerful God with every resource for every believer.

Verses 6-8:
And I will make thee exceeding fruitful, and

> I [Almighty God] will make nations of thee, and kings shall come out of thee.
>
> And I [*El Shaddai,* Almighty God] will establish my covenant between me and thee and thy seed after thee [from Isaac to Christ] in their generations for an everlasting covenant, to be a God [*Elohim*] unto thee, and to thy seed after thee.
>
> And I [*El Shaddai,* Almighty God] will give unto thee, and to thy seed after thee, the land wherein thou art a stranger, all the land of Canaan, for an everlasting possession; and I will be their [thy seed's] God [*Elohim*].

God promised great things to Abraham by giving him the land of Canaan and by assuring Abraham that his offspring would follow *Elohim.*

I want you to note that in chapter 28 of Genesis, Isaac, Abraham's son, called God *El Shaddai.* In the context of this twenty-eighth chapter, Isaac was speaking to his son Jacob.

> Genesis 28:3:
> And God Almighty [*El Shaddai*] bless thee [Jacob], and make thee fruitful, and multiply thee, that thou mayest be a multitude of people.

God Almighty blesses, makes fruitful, and causes our seed to multiply. The Almighty God confirmed with Jacob the same great promise He had given to Jacob's grandfather Abraham.

> Genesis 35:10:
> And God said unto him, Thy name *is* Jacob: thy name shall not be called any more Jacob, but Israel shall be thy name: and he called his name Israel.

God changed Jacob's name. "Jacob" means "supplanter," one who takes the place of another. Instead of "Jacob," God called him "Israel," meaning "prince of God." God's Word says, "Israel shall be thy name: and he called his name Israel."

> Verse 11:
> And God said unto him [Israel], I *am* God Almighty [*El Shaddai*]: be fruitful and multiply; a nation and a company of nations shall be of thee, and kings shall come out of thy loins.

God reiterated to Israel the promise He had made to Abraham, again using the name *El Shaddai*. Associated with that title is fruitfulness, a multitude of nations, and kings from Israel's loins.

> Verse 12:
> And the land which I gave Abraham and Isaac, to thee I will give it, and to thy seed after thee will I give the land.

Do you see the encouragement and knowledge given in the Word of God? Another use of *El Shaddai* is found in Genesis 43 when Israel was speaking to his sons who returned from Egypt.

> Genesis 43:14:
> And God Almighty [*El Shaddai*] give you mercy before the man, that he may send away your other brother, and Benjamin. If I be bereaved *of my children,* I am bereaved.

In this use, Israel was pleading for the mercy of "God Almighty" to deliver his two sons: Simeon and Benjamin.

Genesis 49 speaks of Almighty God's blessings on Joseph.

> Genesis 49:25:
> *Even* by the God of thy father, who shall help thee; and by the Almighty [the Aramaic

text says "Almighty God"], who shall bless thee with blessings of heaven above, blessings of the deep that lieth under, blessings of the breasts, and of the womb.

The Almighty God is the fathomless fountain of living waters, completely bountiful. Not only do the words "Almighty God" denote bountifulness, but they also show blessing. He is a God Who supports His people. He is a God Who defends His people. He is a God Who takes care of His people. The Almighty God is able to and wants to supply every need of every believer.

So the words "Almighty God" and "God Almighty" as they appear in God's Word are always in the context of bountifulness to the believer, blessing to the believer, support to the believer, defense for the believer, supply for the believer's every need. This was the Word of God Almighty to the Old Testament believer. And this is the Word of God for born-again believers since the day of Pentecost, the age of which you and I are a part. The Almighty God has not changed His promise, for we also are Abraham's seed by believing.

You see, there are two classifications of the seed of Abraham: bloodline and believing.

> Galatians 3:7:
> Know ye therefore that they which are of faith [believing], the same are the children of Abraham.

We who believe God are children of Abraham. Therefore, we have the promise of God for bountifulness, for blessing, for support, for defense, for the supplying of needs. The same promise which was made by the Almighty God to Abraham is available to us as children of Abraham because of our believing.

> Galatians 3:28 and 29:
> There is neither Jew [Judean] nor Greek, there is neither bond nor free, there is neither male nor female: for ye are all one [born again of God's Spirit] in Christ Jesus.
>
> And if ye *be* Christ's, then are ye Abraham's seed, and heirs according to the promise.

This "promise" in verse 29 dates back to God's promise to Abraham in Canaan. It is still true to this very day and will continue to be so until the return of Christ.

When you confessed with your mouth the Lord Jesus and believed God raised him from the dead, you were saved. That made you a son of

God and a child of Abraham by believing. We as the believers' line are children of Abraham. And we have the same God Almighty that Abraham had—a God of bountifulness, a God of blessing, a God of support, a God Who defends us, and a God Who supplies our every need.

> Philippians 4:19:
> But my God shall supply all your need according to his riches in glory by Christ Jesus.

This is the same God as the Almighty God of Abraham Who supplied all of Abraham's need and promised to do the same for Abraham's seed as well. How far below par we as sons of God have lived! We need to understand what it means to be children of Abraham. We need to dare to believe the Word which says that our God today is as He was to Abraham. He is still a God of bountifulness and still a God of blessing. He is not a God Who punishes people or denies them. *El Shaddai* is a God Who so loves that He gave His only begotten Son, Jesus Christ, for our redemption so that we could have God in Christ in us, the hope of glory.

II Corinthians 6 says we are workers together with this same God.

II Corinthians 6:1:
We then, *as* workers together *with him* [that
is, with God]. . . .

We work together with God. God is our
employer; He's our boss.

II Corinthians 6 also tells us the kind of people
with whom we should have fellowship.

II Corinthians 6:14:
Be ye [believers, Abraham's seed] not unequally yoked together with unbelievers: for
what fellowship hath righteousness with unrighteousness. . . .

We believers are not to align ourselves in relationships with unbelievers. Righteousness and
unrighteousness simply don't mix. They are
unequal and, in God's eyes, cannot be yoked
together.*

---

*"Unequally yoked" in Greek is the word *heterozugountes*
which means "diversely yoked" or "yoked with another
who is different." This refers to the practice of putting a
yoke on two animals. A farmer would not yoke an ox and
an ass together to help pull a wagon (Deuteronomy 22:10).
They are different kinds of animals and could not pull
smoothly. Likewise Christians who are righteous are to
"pull together" with each other, not with the unrighteous.
Then they can work in harmony.

...and what communion hath light with darkness?

As a believer, you are light. What communion, or fellowship, do you as light have with an unbeliever, who is darkness?

Verses 15 and 16:
And what concord [agreement] hath Christ with Belial [the Devil]? or what part hath he that believeth with an infidel?

And what agreement hath the temple of God [the Body of believers] with idols? for ye [the Body of believers] are the temple of the living God; as God hath said, I [God] will dwell in them, and walk in *them;* and I will be their God, and they shall be my people.

As Almighty God promised to bless Abraham's seed, so He promises to bless the Church of the Body, Abraham's believing line.

Verses 17 and 18:
Wherefore come out from among them [the unbelievers who are trying to tamper with your life and tell you what to do], and be ye separate, saith the Lord, and touch not the

unclean *thing;* and I [the Lord Almighty] will receive you,

And will be a Father unto you, and ye shall be my sons and daughters [those who are born again], saith the Lord Almighty.

There it is—Lord Almighty. This is the same Almighty God Who spoke in Genesis. God says to the Body of believers in the Church today, "I am your Lord Almighty, the Almighty God. I will be bountiful unto you. I will bless you. I will support you. I will defend you. I will supply your every need." This is the significance of the words "Almighty God" in God's Word—not just to Abraham, but from Abraham all the way through to the Body of Christ, the Church, of which you and I are a part.

I began this study by saying that some people are willing for God to be the God of heaven, but not the God on earth, because *they* want to be the God on earth. But some day God Almighty is going to be the one totally in charge. This era in which we live is called "Man's Day" in God's Word. Man does the judging. But the "Lord's Day" is coming; and when it arrives, the will of God shall indeed be done. And at that time the same Almighty God of all bountifulness to us will then deal with the unbeliever.

Revelation 19:11-15:
And I [the Apostle John] saw heaven opened, and behold a white horse; and he that sat upon him *was* called Faithful and True, and in righteousness he doth judge and make war.

His eyes *were* as a flame of fire, and on his head *were* many crowns; and he had a name written, that no man knew, but he himself.

And he *was* clothed with a vesture dipped in blood: and his name is called The Word of God.

And the armies *which were* in heaven followed him upon white horses, clothed in fine linen, white and clean.

And out of his mouth goeth a sharp sword, that with it he should smite the nations: and he shall rule them with a rod of iron: and he treadeth the winepress of the fierceness and wrath of Almighty God.

Almighty God, Who to the believer is bountiful, protective, and supportive, a supplier of the believer's every need, is the same Almighty God Who one day will bring wrath and vengeance upon the unbelievers. This same God will take sweeping action against His enemies. His Son

Jesus Christ is coming back some day as king of kings and lord of lords.

> Verse 16:
> And he hath on *his* vesture and on his thigh a name written, KING OF KINGS, AND LORD OF LORDS.

The Christ who was promised to Abraham is the same Christ who is our lord and savior today. And he is the same Christ Jesus who is going to gather us together and then will come back in judgment, representing Almighty God upon the earth.

After all the reassurances of blessings the Almighty God has given us, surely we can trust in God's almighty ability and allow Him to guide our lives and supply our every need. Truly God is almighty from everlasting to everlasting.

Chapter Two

GOD'S BLUEPRINT OF CREATION

God alone conceived, designed, and ordered life—all of it, from man to the earth to the entire universe. Only His mind could conceive it; only His power could create it; and only His ability could achieve it.

Then God, by way of His Son Jesus Christ, was able to beget spiritual children. Those of us born again of God's Spirit are these children whom God begot because of Christ's works. And we make up a family which is called the family of God, with God as our Father.

The interrelationship of the Father with His family is the very core of Christianity. Christianity is the way of a Father with His family. God is our Father; we are His children. We are members of His family and of His household. And He has already prepared a tremendous home where throughout all eternity we, God's family, can be together.

True Christianity is not a religion. Religions

are man-made; Christianity is what God wrought by Christ Jesus when spiritual sonship became available to mankind.

Not only is Christianity not a religion, it is not a philosophy either. Philosophy is man's wisdom. The German word for "philosophy" is *Weltweisheit*. *Welt* means "world"; *Weisheit* is "wisdom." "World wisdom" is philosophy. Christianity is not world wisdom, but a divine-human relationship.

Not only is Christianity not a religion or a philosophy, it is also not a theology. Theology is the "science of God." For man to explain God would be like having the Model T explain Henry Ford. Man cannot begin to describe the fullness of God's nature and ability. So Christianity could not be a science of God, but rather the union of God and His children.

Twenty-three miles northwest of Camp Gunnison in Colorado, there is a little town known as Irwin, previously called Ruby Camp.*

---

*I've read a diary by H.C. Cornwell which covers the years from 1879 to 1886 at Ruby Camp, a mining camp. The silver mined there was actually a sulfide of silver. It had a crystal form that when crushed was a bloodred color; thus the name "Ruby Camp."

In the spring of 1879 something very exciting occurred at Ruby Camp. The driver of a freight wagon bringing supplies from the railroad came in early one morning. Workmen unloaded his wagon, but he didn't want to leave until the following morning. Since the driver had nothing to do that particular day except wait, he told some people who were standing around that he was thinking about mining a little for himself. The people he spoke to thought they would have some fun with him and advised him, "If you want to find a mine, go down that gully and just start digging; you'll find one."

The wagon driver followed the people's suggestion which was meant as a joke. Less than 400 yards from where he stood that morning, he started digging. To everyone's amazement, he began to see the outcrop of a silver vein. As he continued digging, he found what he later named the "Forest Queen Mine." A short time after he discovered this mine, the man sold it for $50,000. Within two years the buyers took out of that vein silver ore worth one million dollars.

Hundreds of miners had walked over that mine before, but no one had realized the tremendous treasure so close at hand. None had found it except this one man, who named it "Forest Queen."

The Forest Queen Mine is like God's Word. The treasures of God's Word have been available for centuries. The reason people never find its treasures is that they never dig, never search, at the right place. A person cannot know the greatness of God by his five senses. In order to understand spiritual things a person must have the spirit of God within.* Now the Word of God is the most remarkable document in the whole world. Even though God's written Word is in the senses realm, a man who believes it can receive holy spirit and begin to understand the spiritual realm.

For the most part, people never see the greatness of God's Word because they are "natural" people, people without God's spirit. The natural man never will understand God's Word; he simply cannot understand it. I wouldn't criticize a blind man for his analysis of a great masterpiece of art, would I? So why criticize a natural man for his blind attempt to analyze the spiritual truths in the greatest masterpiece of all time, the Word of God?

---

*I Corinthians 2:14: "But the natural man receiveth not the things of the Spirit of God: for they are foolishness unto him: neither can he know *them,* because they are spiritually discerned."

24

W.W. Kinsley, in describing the masterpiece of God's Word, wrote the following:

> *The more profoundly phenomena have been studied by scientists and scientific philosophers the more gloriously have shown out the truths...that God has busied Himself through untold ages in preparing for man's advent, that man has been the grand goal of His endeavor, the ultimate Thule of His creative thought on this planet; that all this prolonged preparation could not have been merely to render comfortable a short-lived and low-planed animal existence; that this patient approach could not have been to a consummation so inconsequential and unworthy.... ***

Blind chance was not the author of life. Explore the mineral kingdom; explore the animal kingdom; explore the vegetable kingdom. From the lowest to the highest, there are marks that specifically call our attention to the superbly conceived reality of that which we observe. Some

---

*E.W. Kenyon, *The Father and His Family,* 11th ed. (Seattle: Kenyon's Gospel Publishing Society, 1964), p. 18, citing W.W. Kinsley.

great design, some great intelligence confronts us everywhere we look in the realm of creation. We can always see an intelligent purpose behind this realm, which was brought about by some type of consistent power.

Take a microscope, even a low-powered one. Focus under its lens an eyeglass, for example. You would see some imperfections in the glass, although perhaps only a few. Next, focus a high-powered microscope on the same eyeglass. You will find that the more high-powered the microscope, the greater the imperfections that will be seen in the glass. There are imperfections in anything man-made.

This example of the eyeglass demonstrates a principle. The more high-powered the microscope used to observe the works of man, the more imperfect the object appears. On the other hand, the more high-powered the microscope used to look upon something that God formed or made, the more perfect and orderly it appears. The closer the scrutiny of God's Word, the more obvious become its beauty and perfection. It is only a man who uses a poor microscope who never sees the greatness of God's Word. He does not observe it to see its perfection.

The Word of God is for all believers the blueprint of creation. God's plan of life to the last finishing touch is intricately set forth in the greatness of His wonderful Word. But a person must be born again to understand it and be willing to renew his or her mind to the truth of that Word, rather than accept man's opinions, religions, philosophies, and theologies.

I Corinthians 2:14 says, "But the natural man receiveth not the things of the Spirit of God...." If natural man does not receive spiritual things from God, then he does not have them. No matter how sincere the natural man looks, no matter how highly educated he may be, or how sensitive, intelligent, and tolerant, he is still a natural man; and the natural man simply cannot receive the things of the Spirit of God "for they are foolishness unto him: neither can he know *them,* because they are spiritually discerned."

The senses man may learn a great deal about the universe in which he lives, but he cannot learn anything about the Creator of that universe. The natural man may see structural design in the universe, but he will never be able to see the Intelligence behind all creation: God. A person can look at a watch and observe that there

27

must be some kind of intelligence behind it. A natural man can do the same with the universe. But the natural man can never see the Intelligence Itself because that takes spirit to understand.

The question "Why creation?" must be the first question answered when a person truly wants to understand God in relation to himself or the world in relation to himself or the universe in relation to himself. The highest sounding of theologies has never given us a reason for creation. Theology, because it lacks a foundation, simply suspends a massive structure of thought and opinion in midair. Theology has given us several cosmological arguments for the existence of God, but it has not given us the simply-stated Biblical answer.

Theologians, for the most part, have found more pleasure in abstract theology than in personal dealings with God. They have found more joy in metaphysics than in divine revelation. Most theologians have founded their positions upon the opinions of men rather than on the Word of God. Theologies and philosophies need constant revitalizing in order to survive. Truth is eternal. Have you ever met a person who was considering revising mathematical tables? Why not? Because they need no revision. Theories, including Darwin's, must constantly be revised and updated. The first three chapters of Genesis have been scoffed at for centuries, and yet it is only those first three chapters that give the truth answering the question "Why creation?" To see the purpose of the universe, we must go to the first chapter of Genesis.

> Genesis 1:14:
> And God said, Let there be lights in the firmament [the expanse] of the heaven to divide the day from the night; and let them be for signs, and for seasons, and for days, and years.

Without those lights in the firmament, the earth would have no days and nights, or seasons and years.

> Verse 15:
> And let them be for lights in the firmament of the heaven to give light upon the earth: and it was so.

The earth was not made to give light to the universe or even to itself; the "lights in the firmament of the heaven" were made to give light to the earth.

29

Verses 16 and 17:
And God made two great lights; the greater
light to rule the day, and the lesser light to
rule the night: *he made* the stars also.

And God set them in the firmament of the
heaven to give light upon the earth.

Notice the earth is God's central focus in His
creative plan. Up to this point in Genesis 1,
everything was made for the earth.

Verses 18 and 19:
And to rule over the day and over the night,
and to divide the light from the darkness:
and God saw that *it was* good.

And the evening and the morning were the
fourth day.

The great star-spangled universe was designed
to support the earth. What then was the earth
designed for? Genesis 1 reveals that the earth was
made to support the physical part of man.

Genesis 1:28-30:
And God blessed them [Adam and Eve],
and God said unto them, Be fruitful, and
multiply, and replenish the earth, and subdue it: and have dominion over the fish of

the sea, and over the fowl of the air, and over every living thing that moveth upon the earth.

And God said, Behold, I have given you every herb bearing seed, which *is* upon the face of all the earth, and every tree, in the which *is* the fruit of a tree yielding seed; to you it shall be for meat.

And to every beast of the earth, and to every fowl of the air, and to every thing that creepeth upon the earth, wherein *there is* life, *I have given* every green herb for meat: and it was so.

The earth was designed to physically support man. God made the earth for man. The heavenly bodies, the animals, the fruit of the trees—these were all made for man. The reason for the earth is man. So then what is the reason for man? God.

Ephesians 1:4-6:
According as he hath chosen us in him before the foundation of the world, that we should be holy and without blame before him in love:

Having predestinated us unto the adoption of children by Jesus Christ to himself, according to the good pleasure of his will,

31

To the praise of the glory of his grace, wherein he hath made us accepted in the beloved.

God created man for Himself, so that He could have companionship, so that He could have children with whom to communicate.

Psalm 8 contains a wonderful revelation of the position God has given His children in His plan.

Psalms 8:5:
For thou hast made him [man] a little lower than the angels, and hast crowned him [man] with glory and honour.

The word translated "angels" is *elohim,* the Hebrew word for "God." So what Psalms 8:5 is really telling us is that God made man a little lower than Himself. That's how well-placed man was intended to be. That demonstrates the greatness of man as the pinnacle of God's creation.

Many years ago when I was reading E.W. Kenyon's *The Father and His Family,* I became totally absorbed in considering his insight about creation, and I would like to share a passage from his book with you now. He noted the record of a well-known astronomer who was discussing with his son the influence of the heavenly bodies on the earth. The following is what the astronomer said to his son.

> *I have noticed that at certain times the Earth is lifted out of her orbit or path by an unseen body lying beyond the reach of our most powerful telescope. If ever they build a larger telescope, I wish you would go and search the heavens to find out what it is that so affects this planet of ours.* *

Kenyon then goes on to say,

> *When the great Lick Observatory was reared with its powerful telescope this son traveled across sea and continent, and one clear night turned the great telescope against the dark space in the heavens where this unseen, uncharted planet reached down its mighty hand and gripped the Earth.*
>
> *After gazing awhile, suddenly there appeared a tiny speck of light; it was a star swinging in its giant orbit away out on the frontier of the Universe.*

---

*Kenyon, *The Father and His Family,* p. 22.

He saw the planet that had so strangely affected the earth. It was millions of miles beyond the farthest star that the human eye had ever seen.

Yet, this giant star sweeping on its great orbit came regularly every few years close enough to our planet, so that it could reach its mighty hand of gravitation down through the unmeasured space and grip our little earth and lift it out of its orbit.

As a ship on the ocean responds to the slightest touch of the helm, our Earth responds to the touch of that distant sentinel and veers swiftly out of its course; then when the planet's grip is loosed, back into its path it comes and goes rhythmically on its way.

This establishes one fact: that there is neither planet, nor sun, nor moon, nor star in all the vast universe but has its influence upon this little planet of ours.

How it thrills the heart to realize that this Earth of ours, so small that one thousand of them can be lost in the sun, is the center and reason for the Universe.

Tonight this old Earth of ours is being held

as safely in the embrace of those uncounted and uncharted planets as a child in its mother's arms.

The heavens are tonight Earth's only perfect timepiece; no watch or clock ever built by man can give us perfect time; but he who knows the path of the stars knows that every star, or sun, or planet will pass a certain given point in the great unpathed space on schedule time.

The star may not have been seen for thousands of years, but she will appear at the cross-roads of the heavens not one second ahead nor one second behind her schedule.

Oh! the wonder of the Architect, the marvel of the Creator, the might of the Sustainer of this great universe of ours!

If the Earth is the reason for the stellar heavens, what is the reason for the Earth?

Before the Morning Stars sang their first anthem to the heart of the lonely Father God, before the foundations of the Earth were laid, before the first rays of light ever passed through the dark expanse, the heart of the great Creator God had a yearning, deep, mighty, eternal.

It was the primordial passion for children.

The Father heart of the Creator God longed for sons and daughters.

This yearning passion took form, and God planned a universe for His Man, and in the heart of that universe He purposed a Home.

There is no time with God.

Time belongs to day and night, to sun and moon.

The Omnipotent God was not hampered by days, nor nights, nor years.

When Love laid the foundations of this mighty universe, He planned, He purposed it all to be the Home of His Man.

It was to be Man's birthplace, Man's Garden of Delight, Man's University where he would learn to know his Father God. *

God said that the earth is the reason for the universe. Man is the reason for the earth. And God is the reason for man. Why did God do all this? The reason is very simple: God wanted sons to love Him, and He wanted daughters to love Him—not by compulsion, not out of necessity, but because of their desire to do so. God so loved

---

*Kenyon, *The Father and His Family,* pp. 22, 23.

that He gave, so that we in turn can love Him and live our lives for Him. God's heart yearns for children. He craves sons and daughters who will freely love Him. Before God had children, He had angels to minister to Him as servants. But He still wanted children. So with love's wonderful, guiding hand, God prepared the earth and the heavens for His children.

If this be true, and I believe it is true according to God's Word, then man is the most wonderful of all of God's creation. And everything in the earth and in the universe is for the person who is God's child. Unbelievers also partake of the blessings of the universe and of the earth, but these blessings were not designed for unbelievers. The blessings were designed for God's children. If God so wanted children and so loved sons and daughters that He spent ages in preparation for them, what a wonderful place those children must hold in His heart and in His eternity. You, as a believer, a son or daughter of God, are the culmination of God's dream because you are God's man, God's woman. The earth was made for you. You were made for God. He is your Father Who loves you. This is God's blueprint of creation.

Chapter Three

HEIRS TOGETHER OF THE GRACE OF LIFE

I do not expect that this chapter will agree with the philosophy of any secular magazine—because the information of the world, of which any secular magazine is a part, is not based on God or His Word. But for those people who want to hear the truth of God's Word, it is our opportunity and our joy to present it to them. Then if they want to believe and obey it, wonderful. Those of us who are already initiated in God's Word know from experience that the only things that ever live for us and that really work in our lives are those things which are built upon the reality of God's wonderful Word.

Now Genesis 2:7 says, "And the Lord God formed man *of* the dust of the ground, and breathed into his nostrils the breath of life; and man became a living soul." The Lord God formed man. When God formed man, He knew what He was doing. It seems to me if God was not satisfied with how He formed man, He would have re-formed him or done whatever was necessary to get man to the place that God was satisfied with His own handiwork.

God made man as He desired. Now it's our job to find out *why* God did it. We need to go to the Word to see what God said man is all about, what woman is all about, and then to get our minds lined up with what the Word says. We shouldn't expect God to get lined up with what V.P. Wierwille or somebody else might want to think. But V.P. Wierwille and everyone else must line themselves up with what the Word says is the reason God formed both man and woman.

Verse 15 of this same second chapter of Genesis says, "And the Lord God took the man, and put him into the garden of Eden to dress it and to keep it." So the Lord God not only formed man, Adam, but He gave man a very definite responsibility. Adam was given a job.

God said He put man in the Garden to dress and to keep it. Where did we ever get the idea that Adam had nothing to do in the Garden of Eden? That is fiction. God put Adam in the Garden of Eden and said, "Look, go to work. Keep busy caring for the Garden and keeping it productive."

Adam had a responsibility to work in the Garden of Eden. Now if a contemporary government decides to financially support its citizens who do not work for that support, that's its privilege. But that's not God's order for the Christian man and woman in our world. God planned for mankind to work. My Bible says that if a person is able but not willing to work, that person shouldn't eat.* God planned for man to work. This was one of God's guidelines. A person never feels so good as when he or she can work. It's a wonderful joy, and it's a privilege to be able to work—to have strength and health and life so we can work. The time to complain is when a person is sick or incapacitated and cannot work. Then a person has something to complain about. But to be able to work is a wonderful privilege and one of man's needs. There are adults who are in business, who work in shops, in factories, on farms, in the home, who know that it's a privilege to work, joyfully living the greatness of God in their lives.

Look at Genesis 2:18. Did the Lord God say, "It's ideal for man to be alone"? No, He said,

---

*II Thessalonians 3:10: "For even when we were with you, this we commanded you, that if any would not work, neither should he eat."

"*It is* not good that the man should be alone; I will make him an help meet for him." A helpmeet, or helpmate, is a companion and helper. The word "companion" means "one who works alongside." God said He would make for man a helpmate, a companion. She's not "just a housewife."* She's a companion, one standing alongside of—not one standing underneath, not one who is a slave to her husband, children, or home.

Notice also that God gave man a *woman* as a companion. He didn't design another man for Adam. He didn't form men for men or women for women. Where did we ever get that idea? It comes from the culture Satan is trying to promote, that every adult has the right to say what is "right" for himself or herself. This certainly isn't what God's Word declares. The Word of God teaches us what is right, and it says that man

---

*It disturbs me when I hear a believing woman say that she is "*just* a housewife." Just a housewife?! That's a disgrace. No woman of God is *just* a housewife. That kind of teaching has pulled some of our very roots out from under us. Women think they're slaves just because they wash the dishes or clean the floors or keep the house in order. I should say not. You're wonderful women born again of God's Spirit, and you've got a tremendous opportunity. You're not "just a housewife." You're a woman with a ministry, a mission, a purpose in life.

42

was made for woman and woman was made for man. And if you don't like it, you ought to call up the Management and complain to Him. He's the one Who designed the pattern.

Generally a man is happiest when he has a woman who will stand with him, someone who is a companion to him. The woman brings out the best there is in her companion. The thirty-first chapter of Proverbs talks about the virtuous woman—her qualities and attributes. One of the characteristics of a virtuous woman is that she is blessed because her husband sits with the elders at the gate; in other words, she is blessed because her husband is a success. And every time he succeeds, she succeeds. It is she who really controls the life stream, not only of the man, but of the whole family. Yet the man is to be the head in that family—not to lord it over the wife, but to be the leader, the one who sets the example, the one who says, "Look, this is what will bless our family." It's the father who puts that spiritual depth in his family.*

Now, God made Eve as a companion to Adam. That means that a woman's primary

---

*For family responsibilities and relationships see Ephesians 5:22-25; 6:1-4; I Peter 3:1-8.

43

responsibility is to help and be a companion to
her man. At no place in the Word of God does it
say that a wife is just a childbearing machine.
That is a denominational teaching. That's all. To
have a child in a family is a blessing, but that
isn't the primary purpose of marriage. The
primary purpose is companionship: having
someone to converse with, someone to understand, someone to love, someone with whom to
pursue goals.

I advise young people not to have children for
two or three years after getting married. Even if
they're thirty when they get married, they can
still have babies at thirty-three. One of the
reasons I advise newlyweds to wait a period of
time before having children has to do with our
American culture. In Biblical times a newly married couple went on a yearlong honeymoon. During that year they accepted no invitations from
anyone except the immediate family on both
sides. During this honeymoon year the couple
could then learn to live with each other and to
know each other better. They also learned to get
along with the in-laws. Not a bad idea!

In contemporary American culture, people get
engaged today, married tomorrow, and the
following day each one goes to a separate job.

She goes to work at four in the afternoon until twelve at night; he goes from eight in the morning until four in the afternoon. And so two people live together for twenty years, have two or three children, and still are strangers to each other. Isn't that something? That's why I advise our newlyweds to get to know each other first before starting a family. The husband and wife need an opportunity to build their companionship. If a child comes in the first year of marriage, it will be a challenge to bring that marriage together. I think all of us know many families who have children, but lack a companionship between husband and wife. And in that companionship is found the sweetness of the life that God intended.

So the first requirement of a marriage is companionship. And if you're going to have companionship, you've got to be able to talk. The husband can't say something and the wife immediately get angry; or the wife can't say something and the husband get upset and storm out of the house. You've got to be able to communicate, have talking sessions. You have to be able to sit down and talk things over. If you don't have time or if you don't take time to communicate, you just cannot put a Christian family together. Exactly what do a husband and wife learn sitting

45

in front of a television set all night watching an outer space movie or a situation comedy? How do a husband and wife learn to communicate if they sit and watch television? It would be better for a couple to sit on a sofa and hold hands and look into each other's beautiful eyes and simply say, "Honey, I think you're the sweetest person." At least that would get a reaction, and it wouldn't be the TV causing it. You see, you've got to have time to talk. You need to have time to relate to one another.

Another dimension that needs to be emphasized in a Christian marriage is the awareness of each other's presence, knowing that the other person is nearby. Sometimes the husband is aware that the wife is in the kitchen while he's in the garage. Just to be aware of her presence gives a husband pleasure. It's just the knowledge that the other is nearby. That's why a husband can't call "the boys" every night and say, "Hey, George, let's go bowling." Tomorrow night, "Hey, Herman, let's go bowling." When you get married, you aren't marrying the fellows you've been bowling with. In a Christian family you married your spouse, and you should spend time building and maintaining that relationship.

Genesis 2:24 says, "Therefore shall a man

leave his father and his mother, and shall cleave unto his wife: and they shall be one flesh." A man and woman don't become this "one flesh" on the first occasion they have sexual relations. "One flesh" means to bring two individuals with different minds, different backgrounds, different mothers and fathers, into a relationship where those two mold their lives together so they become as though one person, acting in unison.

Somebody said that marriage would be much easier if it were like the old wagon—just one tongue. Sorry; there happen to be two tongues: his and hers. A husband and wife can't become one flesh and be molded together unless they want to be and unless they spend time achieving it.

Genesis 2:24 says that a man is to leave father and mother. So, Dad and Mom, let him go! You managed when you got married. Maybe your son and his bride can manage, too, if you don't put pressure on their relationship.

When a man and a woman get married, they ought to move out of Dad and Mom's house. To live with the parents and to work out of the parents' home is not the Biblical way of marriage. A married man and woman have a right to make their own life and their own decisions and grow together in one flesh. And if they live with parents, there will be an extra challenge because the Word says that they're to leave father and mother.

Furthermore, parents should stay out of family arguments. If the new wife can't burn the toast correctly, let her learn. Mother or mother-in-law doesn't have to go over to the newlywed's home and burn the toast. Look, if you have to teach her how to burn the toast after she's married, what kind of mother were you before she got married? You mean to tell me you didn't teach her anything before she was married; but now after she's married, you want to go over and run the family? Let those young people work it out. And then the first time the young wife calls and says, "We're not getting along so good," you say, "Look, Honey, burn your own toast." That's right.

The twenty-eighth verse of Genesis 1 says that God blessed man and woman. And then God said to the man and woman that they should "be fruitful, and multiply, and replenish the earth, and subdue it." And He said they were to "have dominion over the fish of the sea, and over the fowl of the air, and over every living thing that moveth upon the earth." Man and woman were made to have dominion. They cannot have dominion if they are always at odds with each other. When a husband and wife are not in agreement, haggling with each other, they cannot have dominion in the home—over the children, over the environment, over the work in which they are engaged. It's impossible because it's contrary to God's Word.

There will indeed be challenges because there are two heads and two tongues in a marriage. And to build a life together takes the renewed mind with the love of God, putting God first, and communicating with one another.

Without putting God first and having God's Word as a rule book to go by, a marriage can never be put together. People may stay together because it's convenient or because it costs less to stay together than it does to pay alimony or because somebody said that it would be better for the children's sake. None of these reasons deal with the central issue: A true marriage has to be built on God's Word.

In the Christian family God comes first for both the husband and the wife. It is God's will that the husband and the wife put God first and follow Him. Now if a husband doesn't renew his mind to God's Word, what does the wife do?

The wife still has the responsibility of putting God first. Or if a wife doesn't renew her mind to the Word, then what does the husband do? He still has the responsibility of putting God first. That's right! That's the order. God first. Luke 10:27 clearly teaches this: "And he [Jesus] answering said, Thou shalt love the Lord thy God with all thy heart, and with all thy soul, and with all thy strength, and with all thy mind; and thy neighbour as thyself." Love God with all your heart, soul, strength, and mind. That's our highest priority. That's the standard. And the same God that lives in the Christian husband, lives in the Christian wife; therefore, both are to put God first.

So the Christian man and wife have a wonderful opportunity to share their adult lives with each other. As I Peter 3:7 says, a husband and wife are "heirs together of the grace of life." Life is a gift—it's grace, it's to be enjoyed and appreciated. We need to keep this knowledge of life as grace in the forefront of our thinking. You need to think of your spouse as an heir together with you of the grace of life. This attitude will lead your behavior in a godly direction. There will be challenges in the relationship. But it's the challenges with which you are confronted and subsequently work out that make a marriage gratifying. These challenges build depth in a marriage. I do not personally know of two people, even a husband and his wife, who see eye to eye on everything all the time. However, I do believe that two people can so work things out that they can overcome any and every challenge. But, most basic of all, the marriage has to be built on God's Word. It is the Christian family which gives the greatest positive wholeness to life—the companionship and joy and peace and happiness which God intended when He set up the original pattern for man and woman as told to us in the first chapters of Genesis.

PART II

GOD'S ORDER
FOR
LEADERSHIP

GOD'S ORDER FOR LEADERSHIP

Because God is a God of order, He gave specific guidelines with regard to leadership among believers. Chapter 4, "The Qualities of a Spiritual Leader," is a study of the first chapter of Titus. Titus 1 specifies for believers characteristics a person is to demonstrate before that person is designated a leader. God does not simply state once the qualities required for spiritual leadership, but these qualities are again enunciated in the third chapter of I Timothy which is the focus of "The Qualifications for Ordination," thereby establishing and emphasizing these necessary qualities.

Romans 13:1 says that we believers are to be subject to "the higher powers." Many people have erroneously taught that these "higher powers" refer to people in high political positions. Chapter 6, entitled "The Higher Powers of Romans 13," contains the inspiring knowledge that the higher powers are the spiritual leaders within the Body of Christ.

55

Over a period of time, leadership in the Body changes as each generation is born, lives, and dies. So our God provides for orderly succession of leadership within the Body. In "The Transfer of Leadership" we observe Joshua's coming of age. God was preparing Joshua over a period of time to take the responsibilities of leadership at Moses' death.

To know and follow God's guidelines in selecting, ordaining, respecting, and transferring leadership is of great importance. God has not left these issues obscure. He clearly delineates them in His Word so that we can adhere to His instructions and benefit fully by following His way.

Chapter Four

THE QUALITIES OF A
SPIRITUAL LEADER

In the Word of God there are seven books written by the Apostle Paul which are known as the Church Epistles: Romans, Corinthians, Galatians, Ephesians, Philippians, Colossians, and Thessalonians. These are followed by what are referred to as Paul's Pastoral Epistles: Timothy, Titus, and Philemon. And these are followed by the General Epistles by various writers: Hebrews, which was written by Paul, then James, Peter, and John.

In this study I want to observe some truths concerning spiritual leadership that are addressed to us as sons of God in Paul's epistle to Titus. The reason these truths are applicable to our lives is that we, like Titus, are human beings born again of God's Spirit who need personal instruction for our individual relationships with God. The God Who spoke to men and women in Biblical times is still the same God today. Therefore, these scriptures are dynamically revealing

57

to each one of us, and especially to those holding leadership positions in the Church.

Paul begins this epistle to Titus by identifying himself.

> Titus 1:1:
> Paul, a servant of God, and an apostle of Jesus Christ, according to the faith of God's elect, and the acknowledging of the truth which is after godliness.

"Paul, a servant of God...." During the Age of Grace, a person cannot be a servant of God, one who serves God, until after he or she has become a child of God. How can you serve God if you are not born again? You could not serve or participate in your earthly family until you were born into it. So it is with God's family. You must be born again before you can serve God.

Titus is the only epistle in the Bible that Paul's revelation from God was to open with, "Paul, a servant of God." In no other place does he begin an epistle by identifying himself as "a servant of God." And this letter is addressed to a single individual—Titus, a leader in the Church. Paul writes very personally because the one person's life he touches can affect many other people's lives.

Paul's letter continues, "and an apostle." Now an apostle of Jesus Christ is one who is sent by God to bring new light to his generation. Paul brought the new light of the Age of Grace. Paul was an apostle "according to the faith." This faith is the household of faith. The faith that each person receives when he or she is born again is the faith of Jesus Christ. The epistle to Titus goes on to say, "according to the faith of God's elect," of God's chosen, of God's selection. To be selected of God brings up the issue of predestination.

The subject of predestination has a very simple basis, namely, God's foreknowledge. Predestination without foreknowledge would make human beings pawns of God. In fact, some people do indeed explain predestination in this manner, a teaching which is totally erroneous. Our God does not select some of us for heaven and others for hell. Rather, He knows in advance, by foreknowledge, the choices we will make. Each person makes up his or her own mind whether he or she wants to be saved and go to heaven or to stay unsaved and accept the consequences—to believe God or reject Him. But because God knows who will believe and be born again, those individuals were chosen of God before the foundation, or the overthrow,* of the world recorded in Genesis 1.

"Paul, a servant of God, and an apostle of Jesus Christ, according to the faith of God's elect, and the acknowledging of the truth which is after godliness."

"Acknowledging" is "correct and precise knowledge." And "godliness" is our vital spiritual relationship with God because we know the Word of God rightly divided.

An interlinear translation of Titus 1:1 is as follows: "Paul bondman of God, and apostle of Jesus Christ, according to [the] faith of God's elect and knowledge of [the] truth which [is] according to piety."** "According to" indicates "the standard of" and "piety" is "godliness." What a wonderful verse.

> Verse 2:
> In hope of eternal life, which God, that cannot lie, promised before the world began.

---

*Ephesians 1:4: "According as he hath chosen us in him before the foundation [*katabolē,* a throwing down or overthrow] of the world, that we should be holy and without blame before him in love."

***The Englishman's Greek New Testament* (1877; reprint ed., London: Samuel Bagster & Sons, 1970).

At the very moment you were born again, you received eternal life. This eternal life is what God had in mind before He created the heavens and the earth. God, Who neither does lie nor can lie, promised eternal life before the world began. Now the moment you were born again you received eternal life. But could people have eternal life before the day of Pentecost, before it was possible to be born again? Yes, "salvation" was available before the day of Pentecost, but it was not possible to be "born again." In Old Testament times people were saved as they believed in the coming of the Lord Jesus Christ. God reckoned righteousness unto them, as it says in Romans 4:5-9.

Now Peter, Andrew, James, John, Philip, and the rest of Jesus Christ's twelve apostles, plus his numerous disciples, could not be born again during the Gospel period because the new birth was still not available while Jesus Christ walked on the earth. But they could be saved by believing in Jesus as the Messiah, the Son of God. Jesus Christ came to make possible the new birth. It became available after he had ascended and sat down at the right hand of God. Then the plan of salvation was completely complete, so that God was able to make the new birth available on the day of Pentecost.

Once something becomes available, anyone meeting the requirements may have it. Once the new birth was available, anyone who wanted to could be born again. Another example of this truth of availability is the difference between "believing" (or "faith," as the Greek word *pistis* is often translated) and "hope." Believing pertains to those things which are available now. Hope anticipates something which will definitely become available at some point in the future.* Hope relates to something that a person cannot have now but is part of the future, such as Christ's return. We *hope* for Christ's return. It is not yet available.

Titus speaks of the "hope of eternal life." The reason the word "hope" is used is that the fullness of our eternal life is yet future. And the reason we have that future hope is that we belong to God now.

> Titus 1:2:
> In hope of eternal life, which God, that cannot lie, promised before the world began.

---

*Romans 8:24 and 25: "For we are saved by hope: but hope that is seen is not hope: for what a man seeth, why doth he yet hope for? But if we hope for that we see not, *then* do we with patience wait for *it*."

God does not lie; indeed, He cannot lie. And He promised us eternal life. So we can hope for it with certainty throughout all ages.

Verse 3:
But hath in due times manifested his word through preaching...

God manifested His Word, His *logos,* through preaching, or proclaiming. And this still remains the greatest method of outreach for God's Word. Someone must get up and start holding forth the Word of God, word by word and line by line. That is proclaiming, and that is how His Word is manifested so that you can know it.

...manifested his word through preaching, which is committed unto me...

The literal translation of the phrase "which is committed unto me" is "which I was entrusted with." The responsibility of preaching God's Word was entrusted to Paul.

...[which I was entrusted with] according to the commandment of God our Saviour.

The Apostle Paul was entrusted with the preaching of God's Word according to God's commandment. God said, "Paul, you preach." Paul carried this out because it was "the commandment of God our Saviour."

God is our Savior; but His Son, Christ Jesus, is also our savior in that his accomplishments made it possible for us to be reconciled to God. Jesus Christ's work fulfilled God's will for mankind.

> Verse 4:
> To Titus, *mine* own son [true child] after the common faith....

The common faith is the faith that is common to every believer. When we are born again of God's Spirit and belong to the family of God, that's the common household of faith. You have it; I have it; everybody who is born in the family of God has that common faith.

> ...Grace [divine favor], mercy, *and* peace, from God the Father and the Lord Jesus Christ our Saviour.

Now a man can have grace (God's divine favor) and live very ungraciously. He can have the mercy of God, and yet he himself be merciless. He can have the peace of God and live most unpeaceably. That would not be God's fault; that would be man's fault in not recognizing what God has given him and renewing his mind to live accordingly.

The word "Lord" in the phrase "Lord Jesus Christ" does not appear in the majority of critical Greek texts, and the words "Jesus Christ" are inverted. So the entire phrase should simply be "Christ Jesus." The first verse of Titus says "Jesus Christ"; verse 4 says "Christ Jesus." We are servants of Jesus Christ as we minister to people, but we are in Christ Jesus as sons of God. "Jesus Christ" emphasizes Jesus' walk on earth, the humiliated one who served. "Christ Jesus" emphasizes the exalted, glorified Christ, with whom we are exalted.

We can talk about the precision of science, but we haven't truly seen any precision until we look at the perfection of God's matchless Word. That Word sets like a diamond, yet people have by-passed it throughout the years because they couldn't fathom its depth. God's Word is too great.

We are in Christ Jesus who is God's only begotten Son, who had a mission to accomplish. The Word of God says that when he was baptized, we were baptized with him. When he died, we died with him. When he was buried, we were buried with him. When he arose, we arose with him. When he ascended, we ascended with him. When he sat down at the right hand of God, we sat down with him. That is what Jesus Christ did for us.

We are sometimes told to "bear our cross." Who is capable of bearing the cross Christ bore? No one but God's only begotten Son. When the Bible talks about taking up our cross and following him, it is referring to taking up our responsibilities. Jesus Christ died so that we might live. He carried the sins of mankind so that you and I could carry God's love to mankind. We don't have to carry around our sins. No one does. Jesus Christ already carried them. He carried the cross of pain so we could carry the cross of deliverance. He carried the cross of envy so that we could carry the cross of joyful response with love. You see, he carried all of those burdensome things so that you and I could carry all the good and glorious things. He died that we might live. He came that we might have life and have it more abundantly.

> Verse 5:
> For this cause left I [Paul] thee [Titus] in Crete, that thou shouldest set in order the things that are wanting [left undone]....

The churches on Crete, an island in the Mediterranean, were young churches. And Paul said to Titus, "I left you over there in Crete to put in order the things which still needed to be done."

> ...and ordain elders in every city, as I had appointed thee.

Titus was told to ordain elders. "To ordain" is to set people in positions of responsibility. The word "elder" denotes a leader who is not a newcomer, a neophyte, a fledgling, or a pledge. A leader, or elder, is to be someone who has been seasoned, having had time to become rooted in God's Word. The word "elder" describes someone who is older in experience, with more exposure to the truth of God's Word, though chronological age is not mentioned. It does not say that a person has to be as old as Methuselah in order to be an elder; ordination as an elder has to do with one's quality as a believer, not one's age.

The word "elder" in the Old Testament has the same usage as the words "bishop" and "elder" in the New Testament. In other words, the elders of the Old Testament period served the same functions as the bishops and elders in the

New Testament period. The word "elder" emphasizes the dignity of the position, while "bishop" emphasizes the function of the office.

"...Ordain elders in every city...." The Greek literally means "from city to city" or "city by city." Ordination of an elder did not occur in every city. Not every city in Crete had a group of believers. And God's Word, via Paul to Titus, was to ordain a responsible person to run each existing local fellowship, if a believer there were qualified.

Then God's Word in Titus 1 goes on to tell what the requirements of an elder are.

> Verse 6:
> If any be blameless [*anenklētos*]....

This doesn't say "faultless." It says "blameless." None of us is ever going to live without faults, without sins creeping in. But our faults are not of the magnitude to be deserving of accusations; "nothing laid to one's charge" is the meaning in Greek.

> ...the husband of one wife, having faithful [believing, steadfast] children not accused of riot [*asōtia,* looseness of manners and morals] or unruly [*anupotaktos,* insubordinate,

rebellious, disobedient, headstrong, perverse].

A leader is to have only one wife and well-behaved children. If you, as a Christian parent, can't take care of your own offspring, you have no right to lead other people. If you cannot lead your own children and have them respond to you, how can you direct the Body of the Church of God?

> Verse 7:
> For a bishop must be blameless [*anenklētos*], as the steward [*oikonomos*] of God; not selfwilled [*authadēs*]...

A steward of God is a manager of God's household. And the manager of God's household cannot be self-willed, determined to do things his own way.

> ...not soon angry [*orgilos*]...

In the Greek texts there is no word here for "soon." And the word for "angry" is *orgilos* which can be translated "having a buildup of emotion which is allowed to fester to the point of seeking revenge." So one of the qualities of a manager of God's household is that he or she

69

does not become emotional to the point of desiring punishment or revenge.

. . .not given to wine [*mē paroinos*]. . .

That doesn't mean a bishop can't drink a little wine, but it does mean he is to be temperate, moderate, in drinking wine. He is not prone to intemperance. That's what the Word says.

. . .no striker [*plēktēs*]. . .

A leader is not to be quarrelsome or pugnacious.

. . .not given to filthy lucre [*aischrokerdēs*].

"Filthy lucre" refers to the love of money. There's nothing wrong with money itself. It's not money that is the root of all evil. I Timothy 6:10 says that it's the *love* of money that is the root of all evil. Why? Because a person who loves money can never get enough of it, and money becomes a goal in itself instead of a means to a worthy goal.

The Greek word translated "given to filthy lucre" literally means "greedy of dishonorable gain or base advantage." A steward of God is not to be greedy for dishonorable gain.

Verses 6 and 7 of Titus 1 itemize some of the qualities an elder or bishop is to avoid. Now, verses 8 and 9 list the qualities a bishop should demonstrate.

Verse 8:
But a lover of hospitality [*philoxenos*]...

An elder, or bishop, is one who loves to be hospitable, who is kind to strangers, and who makes welcome those who enter his home.

...a lover of good men [*philagathos,* good things]...

The text reads "a lover of good [things]." In other words, a bishop should be a lover of what is good. Many Bibles have the word "things" in the center reference.

...sober [*sōphrōn*]...

The text literally means "of a sound mind." The added nuances of being sound-minded are to be discreet, sane, curbing one's desires and impulses, self-controlled.

...just [*dikaios*], holy [*hosios*], temperate [*enkratēs*].

The Greek word for "just" means "equitable," "honest," or "fair." "Holy" means "undefiled by sin and wickedness." The Greek word for "temperate" means "having strong mastery of self." Thus a leader is to be fair, undefiled, and master of himself or herself.

> Verse 9:
> Holding fast the faithful word. . . .

To hold fast the faithful Word means that we don't let anybody talk us out of it; nor do we talk ourselves out of it. The faithful Word must be held fast before it can be held forth in teaching.

> Verse 9:
> Holding fast the faithful word as he hath been taught, that he may be able by sound doctrine [right believing] both to exhort and to convince [*elenchō,* convict, refute] the gainsayers.

A Greek interlinear translation reads, "Holding to the faithful word according to the teaching, that he may be able both to encourage with sound teaching, and to convict those who gainsay."* The word "teaching" is "doctrine"

---

*The Englishman's Greek New Testament.

and "sound" is "uncorrupt." Elders are to cleave to God's Word so that by uncorrupt doctrine they can exhort anyone listening, and they can convict or refute gainsayers, or contradictors. How can you convict the contradictors? By sound doctrine, by errorless teaching. A leader can both encourage people and invalidate contradictors with sound doctrine.

Verse 10:
For there are many unruly [*anupotaktos*] and vain talkers [*mataiologos*] and deceivers [*phrenapatēs*], specially they of the circumcision [the legalistic Judeans].

Today we have the same kinds of contradictors. Some are unruly, insubordinate, and rebellious. Others are vain talkers, meaning their talk is useless, profitless, and characterized by worthless debates. The contradictors deceive people's minds.

Verse 11:
Whose [the contradictors'] mouths must be stopped [*epistomizō,* muzzled], who subvert [*anatrepō,* overthrow or destroy] whole houses [entire households], teaching things which they ought not, for filthy lucre's

73

[*aischros kerdos,* base or dishonorable gain's] sake.

The unruly people, the vain talkers, and the deceivers cause problems in households; they destroy families with error. And they do it for dishonorable gain. An elder must be able to muzzle such subverters.

Verse 12:
One of themselves, *even* a prophet of their own, said, The Cretians *are* alway liars, evil [wild] beasts, slow bellies [*argos gastēr,* lazy gluttons].

This is no compliment for the people of Crete. One of their own people described his countrymen as liars, beasts, and lazy gluttons. Believers should not be like this; they should be the exact opposite, according to the Word of God.

Verse 13:
This witness [testimony] is true....

Paul says that the observation about those Cretians was accurate. That's the way they were. They were liars and wild beasts and idle gluttons. Therefore, the leaders were to reprove them rigorously, telling them to go to work, to quit being

74

idle, to quit lying, and to stop behaving like wild beasts.

> Verses 13 and 14:
> This witness is true. Wherefore rebuke [*elenchō,* convict, refute] them sharply [*apotomōs,* curtly], that they may be sound in the [family] faith;
> Not giving heed to Jewish [Judean] fables [*muthos,* myths], and commandments of men, that turn from the truth.

The leader was to rebuke the Cretians with directness so that they might be errorless in the household of faith and so that they would not give heed to Judean fables or to the commandments of men which were turning people from the truth.

> Verse 15:
> Unto the pure all things *are* pure: but unto them that are defiled and unbelieving *is* nothing pure; but even their mind [understanding] and conscience is [are] defiled.

In the Greek it is clear that this verse 15 begins a new topic. It literally reads, "All things [are] pure to the pure." God is still advising the leader so that he understands the defiled Cretians. They aren't pure. They are stained and unbelieving, so nothing is pure to them.

> Verse 16:
> They [the defiled and unbelieving] profess that they know God; but in [by] works they deny *him,* being abominable [*bdeluktos,* detestable], and disobedient [*apeithēs,* told the truth but rejected it], and unto every good work reprobate [*adokimos,* worthless].

The impure say that they know God, but by their actions they deny Him because they are detestable, rejecting the truth, and are worthless for every good work.

This is a beautiful chapter in which Paul teaches Titus the basis on which to choose the spiritual leaders of Crete. A good leader is truly a servant—a son of God who chooses to serve God by ministering to men and women. What great qualities an elder, a leader, must have. All of us need to think about these qualities and build the greatness of this knowledge in our minds. Whether or not we are ordained as an elder, each of us should work at developing the sound qualities set forth in Titus 1: blameless, not self-willed, not angry or seeking revenge and desiring to punish, not intemperate, not quarrelsome, not greedy of dishonorable gain, a lover of hospitality, a lover of what is good, of a sound mind, self-controlled, fair and equitable, not defiled or stained by sin and wickedness, and having mastery of self. We must hold to errorless doctrine to encourage the hearers and to refute the contradictors. This great sound doctrine of God's Word has the power of God behind it; it can take men's and women's lives from the valley of mere existence and put them on the high road to glory.

We thank God for setting forth these guidelines for leadership so that we can examine our own lives and walks and set the Word's standards for ourselves.

Chapter Five

THE QUALIFICATIONS FOR ORDINATION

No greater commitment can be made by a man or woman than to accept God's call to ordination. No responsibility exceeds the commitment of a person who is ordained to the Christian ministry. Since ordination is such a momentous responsibility, surely God's Word makes it clear who is qualified to be ordained as a minister of God. What are God's requirements? The previous chapter of this book examined the first chapter of Paul's epistle to Titus, which states the qualities a bishop or leader is to possess. In this chapter, we will make an in-depth study of I Timothy 3 to find out more about the qualifications for ordination.

I Timothy 3:1:
This *is* a true saying, If a man desire the office of a bishop [overseer, elder], he desireth a good work.

"This *is* a true saying" literally reads, "Faithful is the [God's] Word,"* "the Word is faithful." If a person aspires to ordination into a leadership office (or function), he desires something which God calls "good." God approves of a person's desire for a leadership position. After giving such a desire His approval in verse 1, in verses 2-7 God enumerates specific qualifications for this type of leadership.

> Verse 2:
> A bishop [overseer, elder] then must be blameless [*anepileptos*], the husband of one wife, vigilant [*nēphalios*], sober [*sōphrōn*], of good behaviour [*kosmios*], given to hospitality [*philoxenos*], apt to teach [*didaktikos*].

A leader in the Church has to be "blameless." Now this word "blameless" does not at all carry the connotation a reader might assume. "Blameless" in its in-depth meaning denotes that a bishop must be "prepared at all points, so as not to be caught anywhere by an antagonist." The Greek word for "blameless," *anepileptos,* is

---

*This same Greek phrase (*pistos ho logos*) is also used in I Timothy 1:15; 4:9; II Timothy 2:11; Titus 3:8.

used in secular Greek literature of a wrestler who is prepared at all points so that he won't be pinned by an opponent. How does a person become prepared at all points so as not to be caught by an antagonist? By the Word of God. That's why we study to show ourselves approved unto God as workmen who need not to be ashamed, rightly dividing the Word of Truth. What a great responsibility for a candidate for ordination—to be prepared at all points.

Besides being prepared by knowing the Word of God, a bishop is to be "the husband of one wife." I don't know if this statement means that every bishop must have a wife or not; but if so, he is to have only one.

The Greek word for "vigilant" actually means "clearheaded." "Not getting into a problem-situation, including not becoming intoxicated" is denoted. A leader is not an extremist one way or the other. He's stable in all matters. That's the significance of *nēphalios*.

The Greek word for "sober" means "a sound, rational mind to the end that he restrains his passions."

"Of good behaviour" is "well ordered, well behaved, discreet, respectable."

"Given to hospitality" means that a bishop is generous to guests and loving to strangers. It implies that the leader knows how to handle himself or herself, how to be the most gracious host or hostess, how to groom himself or herself, and how to make guests comfortable. That's the word "hospitality."

Then "apt to teach" means "able and skillful in teaching." If a person has natural leadership ability and he does what the Word says, then he'll learn to teach and always be ready to teach.

So, "an overseer must be prepared at all points, a husband of one wife, clearheaded, having a sound mind to the end that he restrains his passions; he is also discreet and respectable, hospitable, and able and ready to teach." That's a literal translation according to usage of verse 2.

> Verse 3:
> Not given to wine, no striker [*plēktēs*], not greedy of filthy lucre [*aischrokerdēs*]; but patient [*epieikēs*], not a brawler [*amachos*], not covetous [*aphilarguros*].

A leader is "not given to wine"; if he drinks, he drinks in moderation. And he is "no striker"—he is not eager to quarrel or pick fights. Neither is he greedy of base gain. But a leader is equitable,

82

fair, and forbearing. A leader tempers strict justice with gentle mercy; that is, he does not show favoritism. This is a very important quality for a bishop to have.

"...Not a brawler...." A "brawler" is one who is contentious, one who always wants to pick a fight. God's leader, however, is not like this. He is disinclined to fight, preferring peace.

"...Not covetous...." The Greek word for "covetous" means "loving money." A leader is not avaricious; he doesn't love money. Money is not a leader's motivating force.

Verse 4:
One that ruleth [*proistēmi*] well his own house, having his children in subjection [*hupotagē*] with all gravity [*semnotēs*].

A leader is one who takes charge in his own house, having his children "in subjection." "Subjection" means "loving obedience." The Greek word for "subjection" is the same word used regarding wives in I Timothy 2:11. Subjection doesn't mean the children are slaves, any more than a wife is. A bishop doesn't mistreat his family, but he has well-behaved children. That's what it means. Children are not to rule the house. A leader's children are to be "in subjection with all

83

gravity," with all respect. The children respect their father.

> Verse 5:
> (For if a man know not how to rule his own house, how shall he take care of the church of God?)

If a man can't manage his own household, how could he oversee the Church of God? He may think he can, and he may put up a convincing front, but the Word of God says he cannot oversee the Body of Christ if he can't first rule his own house well. So either God's Word is right or it's wrong.

> Verse 6:
> Not a novice, lest being lifted up with pride he fall into the condemnation of the devil.

A leader is not to be a novice. "Novice" in Greek is *neophutos,* transliterated into "neophyte." A pledge in a fraternity is a "neophyte." In other words, the ordained leader is not somebody who was just born again last night and ordained as an elder in the Church this morning. Rather, he is someone who has stood faithfully day after day, week after week, and even year after year—until the time is right for him to

84

assume leadership responsibilities. "...Lest being [in order that he be not] lifted up with pride...." "Lifted up with pride" means "puffed up, or conceited." A person who is aged (seasoned) in the Word isn't puffed up with self-importance as a neophyte might be. He is moved neither by praise nor by criticism.

"...Fall into the condemnation of the devil." The word "condemnation" is "judgments." A man puffed up over himself could possibly ("lest") fall into devilish judgments.

> Verse 7:
> Moreover [but] he must have a good report [*martus*]* of them [also] which are without; lest he fall into reproach [*oneidismos*] and the snare of the devil.

A believer is to have a good report from the Body of believers that are outside of his own

---

*The word "report" comes from the Greek word for "martyr," *martus*. *Martus* is related to the Sanskrit root *smr-* or *smarami*, "to remember"; in the Zend language, *mar* signifies to recollect. A witness is one who recollects. When you're brought into court as a witness, you are to recollect or remember. So how did the word "martyr" become associated with blood and death? Because of the Christians who witnessed to their beliefs who were killed (Acts 22:20). The Greek word became anglicized, and a martyr became one who dies for his beliefs.

immediate family. He has to have a good report, a good witness, among the fellow believers. This "good report" has to be among those in the Body over whom he is the overseer.

The word "lest" deals with the consequences for a bishop if he should not have a good report with believers outside his family. If a person who does not meet the requirements or have a good witness were put in a position of leadership, as a bishop—an overseer or elder—that person could "fall into reproach and the snare of the devil." And the word "reproach" means that the leader would begin to be blamed and criticized by believers. The "snare" is a "trap." The bishop could fall into a trap of the Devil. However, so long as a leader walks by the revealed Word of God, he's not going to get in that trap.

Now we have read for ourselves the basic principles of the walk of leadership. These seven verses from I Timothy 3 are some of the primary verses in the Word of God for any man or woman to keep foremost in his or her mind in preparation for leadership responsibilities. Men and women who want to be leaders for God must live by these principles. If they don't, they're going to end up in the snare of the Devil.

Romans 12:1 says, "I beseech you therefore,

brethren, by the mercies of God, that ye present your bodies a living sacrifice...." This means that a believer, and especially a leader, doesn't sleep in until ten o'clock in the morning. A person called of God has to be the first person up in the morning—ready to work, preparing to serve God's people. A leader gets up, prays, reads God's Word, and speaks in tongues; he must be prepared with the greatness of God's Word alive in his heart and mind. After men or women are ordained, they are the ones who have to set the pace; they have to expend the time and energy to be in the vanguard. When men and women are ordained of God, they are responsible to lead God's people. Whatever it takes makes no difference; leaders simply do it. Why? Because they are ordained of God; they are called by and committed to the Highest.

And when God calls leaders, He expects them to stand faithfully on His Word. They have no friends when it comes to the Word, except those friends who want to stand with them on the Word. God's Word has to remain untouched and untarnished because God magnified it above all His name. It's His Word that tells us His will. No man will know the will of God without knowing the Word of God. Anyone can guess. But true believers cannot afford to guess; we're dealing with eternal verities. We're dealing with God. We're dealing with that which will take us throughout all eternity. If God's Word is wrong, then we have nothing. But we do not believe God's Word is wrong; we believe that the Word of God is the will of God—that the Word of God means what it says and says what it means, and that God has a reason for saying what He says—where He says it, how He says it, to whom He says it, when He says it.

A call to service indicates that someone must take care of problems and needs. When a plumber gets a phone call from someone with a plumbing problem, what does he do? He services the call. When an electrician gets a call, what does he do? He services the call. What about servicing the calls of people with spiritual needs—needs that can only be met by God's Word? God has called leaders to serve His people. No matter how much time it takes, no matter what must be done, leaders must respond to the call. They are responsible to God to serve God's people: to pray with them, to love them, to teach them, to minister to them. They simply have to dedicate their entire beings in service to God's people.

The life of an overseer is not an easy one. It's a disciplined walk. And the sole purpose of ordaining men and women is to bless the Body of

Christ, to take care of the Body, so that the Body can function more effectually and more effectively. Ordination is a call to service.

Luke 9 contains an account of Jesus Christ's calling a few people to serve with him. I want to read this record specifically to watch the various reactions to Jesus' call. Luke 9:57 says, "And it came to pass, that, as they [Jesus and his disciples] went in the way, a certain *man* said unto him, Lord, I will follow thee whithersoever thou goest."

Jesus responded to the man by explaining, "Foxes have holes, and birds of the air *have* nests; but the Son of man hath not where to lay *his* head." Jesus Christ's response does not mean that he was poverty-stricken. It means that Jesus moved among the people. He didn't have a place where he stayed day after day, because he was moving about ministering to people.

The man speaking to Jesus said, "Lord, I'll follow you wherever you go." Jesus said, "If you plan to, let me remind you that foxes have their abodes and birds of the air have their nests as homes, but the Son of man has no place where he lives week after week and month after month."

Jesus said to another person, in verse 59 of Luke 9, "Follow me. But he [the man] said,

89

Lord, suffer me first to go and bury my father." This is an orientalism meaning "take care of my family." The man wasn't saying that his father was dead. What he was saying was, "Let me stay at home until my father dies and I've taken care of my family responsibilities, then I'll follow you."

In verse 60, "Jesus said unto him, Let the dead bury their dead...." Everyone knows that the dead can't bury anybody. This orientalism, properly understood, means "Let the city bury the dead." Jesus' reply was, "Let somebody else take care of those responsibilities. I have an even greater responsibility for you. You go and preach the Kingdom of God."

Verse 61 says, "And another also said, Lord, I will follow thee; but let me first go bid them farewell, which are at home at my house." In other words, "Let me go home and say good-bye to all my friends and relatives." Jesus responded to this request in verse 62, "No man, having put his hand to the plough, and looking back, is fit for the kingdom of God."

This statement by Jesus is a fitting message about serving God in ordination. No one who is ordained, who puts his hand to the plow, who accepts God's call to ordination, is fit for the

Kingdom of God if he turns back or longs to return to his life before ordination.

People have all kinds of excuses for a lack of commitment. But there is no acceptable excuse. There is nothing whatsoever that excuses a person from his commitment of ordination. There is no excuse for turning back to one's old ways.

Once you have put your hand to the plow, accepted ordination for God, you must not look back. You must keep moving forward and looking toward that day when our lord and master shall return, when those who are alive and remain shall be changed and the dead in Christ shall rise. That is the long-term, wholehearted commitment to which a person agrees when he or she accepts the call to serve God's people in ordination.

Chapter Six

THE HIGHER POWERS OF ROMANS 13

I want you to be able to understand one chapter of the Bible which very few people do understand, namely, the thirteenth chapter of Romans. This chapter speaks of subjecting ourselves to higher powers. These "higher powers" have been a source of misunderstanding which I want to clarify in this study. As background to Romans 13 and the "higher powers," we need to bear in mind the information given in I Corinthians 12:27 and 28.

> I Corinthians 12:27 and 28:
> Now ye are the body of Christ, and members in particular.
>
> And God hath set some in the church, first apostles, secondarily prophets, thirdly teachers, after that miracles, then gifts of healings, helps, governments, diversities of tongues.

"Now ye are the body of Christ...." The Body of Christ is the Church. We believers are the Body of Christ, and every person in that Body is a member in particular. God is telling us that each person in the Body is special and has a specific function, or ministry, in that Body. When each member of the Body functions with the greatest of his or her God-given ability, each person's spiritual life will be totally full. Then the entire Body of Christ, the Church, will operate with complete perfection.

A person in the Body of Christ has the same rewards available whether he or she serves as a prophet or as an apostle or a teacher or in helps or governments or some other facet of the Church. Those who teach are entitled to no greater reward than those who minister in helps or governments or in any other way. Each of us in the Body of Christ has a particular function in that Body, and we are to function with all our heart, soul, mind, and strength.

Let me give you a literal translation according to usage of verse 28 of I Corinthians 12: "So God has placed some in the Church having the ministries of apostles, prophets, and teachers. Some are effective miracle workers. Some are very effective in imparting the blessings of healings.

94

Some are very adept as helps and governments. And some contribute best with diversity of tongues."

Apostles, prophets, and teachers are gift ministries to the Church. Miracles, healings, and diversities of tongues are manifestations of the gift from the Holy Spirit in the Church. And helps and governments are service ministries in the Church.

Whatever a person's God-given assignment is, he or she must proceed to carry it out. A person can have the ministry of an apostle, a prophet, or a teacher, in helps or governments, or be adept in prophesying, but what profit is it until that ability is put to work? A person may have the ministry of teaching the Word of God, but instead of teaching the Word of God, he just sits and does nothing. Then that ability will not be a benefit to anybody. The Body of Christ is perfected as each person carries out his or her assignment in that Body.

The same truth concerning the functions in the Body is set forth in Romans 12, the context of the thirteenth chapter of Romans, which is the focus of this study.

Romans 12:4:
For as we have many members in one body, and all members have not the same office.

95

The word "office" means "function." All believers do not have the same function in the Body of Christ. Our assignments differ from one another's.

> Verse 5:
> So we, *being* many, are one body in Christ, and every one members one of another.

The reason we're all members one of another is that we're fitly joined together* and interdependent in the one Body. Each individual's function is vitally important.

> Verse 6:
> Having then gifts differing according to the grace that is given to us, whether prophecy, *let us prophesy* according to the proportion of faith [believing].

This verse has a tremendous literal translation according to usage. "Having then *charismata* [spiritual abilities, functions in the Body] differing according to the divine favor that is given to

---

*Ephesians 4:16: "From whom [Christ] the whole body fitly joined together and compacted by that which every joint supplieth, according to the effectual working in the measure of every part, maketh increase of the body unto the edifying of itself in love."

us, whether in the ministry of prophecy, continue prophesying according to the proportion of your believing." Our spiritual abilities are *charismata,* God-given functions.

Verse 7:
Or ministry, *let us wait* on [*en,* in] *our* ministering: or he that teacheth, on [in] teaching.

The words *"let us wait"* are italicized in the King James Version and should be deleted as they are misleading in contemporary English. So, verse 7 should read, "Or ministry, in ministering; or he that teacheth, in teaching."

In context verses 6 and 7 mean that the person who has a God-given ability in prophecy should be actively prophesying. And if another person has a different type of ministry, he or she should get active doing that type of ministering. For example, if you have the ministry of teaching, get busy teaching—do it.

Verse 8:
Or he that exhorteth, on [in] exhortation: he that giveth, *let him do it* with simplicity; he that ruleth, with diligence; he that sheweth mercy, with cheerfulness.

The first part of verse 8 logically belongs with verses 6 and 7: "Whether prophecy, get on with prophesying; or ministry, in ministering; or he that teacheth, in teaching; or he that exhorteth, in exhortation." He or she who has the ministry of exhorting is to be diligent in exhorting.

Then verse 8 should begin with, "He that giveth, *let him do it* with simplicity." The word "simplicity" is the Greek word *haplotēs* which literally means "singleness" or "plainness." Let him who gives do so with simplicity, not with strings attached or with ulterior motives. Never give with the attitude of "what can I get out of it."

He who rules—the word "ruleth" means "presides"—let him preside with diligence, expending zealous effort.

And he that shows mercy is to do it with cheerfulness. "Mercy" is the withholding of judgment when judgment is deserved. The Greek word for "cheerfulness" is *hilarotēs,* from which is derived the English word "hilarity." God says, in other words, that if you're showing mercy to someone, really enjoy it.

Do you know why it is so beautiful and easy to show mercy with cheerfulness? Because all you have to remember is God's mercy to you. When you remember God's mercy to you, then you will never have any difficulty showing mercy with cheerfulness to a brother or sister. When I remember the things for which God forgave me when I deserved judgment, I have no difficulty in forgiving others. But when I get puffed up and forget my own shortcomings for which God has withheld judgment of me, then I become critical of others. So it is with every one of us.

A translation of verse 8 according to usage is: "He that gives in any capacity in the Church let him do it with simplicity; he that presides or takes charge, let him do it with diligence; and he that shows mercy, let him do it with great cheerfulness." See how perfectly this fits? All of the instructions are on attitudes that men and women in the Body of Christ should have as they carry out these benefits among God's people.

Now, in this context of Romans 12, which gives the believer specific instructions regarding functions in the Church, comes this great, and usually misunderstood, thirteenth chapter of Romans.

Romans 13:1:
Let every soul be subject unto the higher powers [*exousia,* exercised authority]. For

there is no power but of God: the powers that be are ordained of God.

"Let every soul [every person, every individual] be subject unto the higher powers...." Usually this is interpreted to mean that the higher powers refer to political governments. This is not and cannot be true. It's very clear as we continue the thought trend of Romans 12 that this first verse of Romans 13 is speaking of the functions within the Body of Christ, the Church. God is not talking about the Congress or the President or the Supreme Court of the United States or those with governmental authority in any nation's political structure. The Word of God here is talking about the Body of believers in relationship to the higher authorities in that Body. Let every soul, every person, be subject unto the higher powers. The higher powers are those operating *charismata,* the spiritual abilities and assignments, which God has set in the Church to help the Body function properly. That is the immediate context of this thirteenth chapter.

"...For there is no power but of God...." Everyone who has this higher authority in the Church received it from God—"...the powers that be are ordained of God." "Power" is translated from the Greek word *exousia,* meaning

"exercised authority." You could never say that
governmental powers are set by God, could you?
But Bible commentators have! They have said
that worldly powers are ordained of God, and
they quote this scripture. That's not at all what is
being spoken of here. This is talking about the
Church, the powers inside the Church. Those to
whom God has given authority for governing the
Body are ordained or appointed of God.

A literal translation according to usage of
Romans 13:1 is: "Every believer is to be quietly
subdued to and lovingly reverent of the higher
powers placed in the Church by God. For there is
no exercised authority in the Body but the specifically and properly designated order of God."

> Verse 2:
> Whosoever therefore resisteth the power
> [the authority that God has set in the
> Church], resisteth the ordinance [*diatagē,*
> order, arrangement] of God: and they that
> resist shall receive to themselves damnation
> [*krima,* judgment].

Here the word "power" again is the word *exousia,* exercised authority. "Ordinance" is the
Greek word *diatagē,* meaning "order, arrangement, setup." The word "receive" is the word

lambanō, "receive to the end of manifesting." "Damnation" is *krima* which means "judgment." A literal translation according to usage of verse 2 is as follows: "The believer in the Body who stands against or sets himself above the exercised authority in the Church either by his word or his action judges himself, for he opposes God's arrangement."

> Verse 3:
> For rulers are not a terror to good works, but to the evil. Wilt thou then not be afraid of the power? do that which is good, and thou shalt have praise of the same.

"Rulers" are those who exercise authority within the Body. The word "terror" is the Greek word *phobos,* meaning "a fear or fright." To "be afraid of the power" is to have respect, reverence, awe for the authority (*exousia*) that God has set in the Church.

The rulers in the Church are instituted to encourage good works and to avoid evil. The believers should reverence those exercising this authority. Believers should do those things which are good and thus receive praise from the rulers.

Verse 4:
For he is the minister of God to thee for good. But if thou do that which is evil, be afraid; for he beareth not the sword in vain: for he is the minister of God, a revenger to *execute* wrath upon him that doeth evil.

"He" is not the minister in a secular government, but this verse is speaking of the higher powers in the Church, those who have exercised authority in the Church. They are ministers of God to bring the benefits of God to God's people—"to thee for good."

"...But if thou do that which is evil, be afraid; for he beareth not the sword in vain...." The "sword" has been said to mean shotguns, army rifles, tanks, bullets. No. What sword does the man of God carry? The Word of God. He brings the Word. He is the minister of God, one who executes justice by reading the evildoer the Word and teaching it to him. The ruler executes justice by showing the Word to the evildoer and declaring, "Thus saith the Lord."

Verses 5 and 6:
Wherefore *ye* must needs be subject, not only for wrath, but also for conscience sake.

For for this cause pay ye tribute also: for they are God's ministers, attending continually upon this very thing.

A literal translation of verse 5 is: "Therefore, you the believer are to be lovingly in reverence and subjection, but not because you know you will be corrected by the Word if not. If you build the Word in your life as a habit pattern, then you will need no correction."

Verse 6 begins, "For for this cause pay ye tribute." You are to give money. One of the reasons you give money is that the rulers in the Church are God's ministers, continually serving God's people according to the Word of God.*

Verse 7:
Render therefore to all their dues: tribute to whom tribute *is due;* custom to whom custom; fear [reverence] to whom fear [reverence]; honour to whom honour.

Is God talking about a secular government? No. He is talking about the higher powers in the

---

*See I Corinthians 9:1-19, especially verse 14: "Even so hath the Lord ordained that they which preach the gospel should live of the gospel."

104

Body of Christ, the Church. Give to God's ministers whatever is due them, whether it be tribute, custom, reverence, or honor.

Be sure you are giving to the higher powers in the Body all that is due them. It is a terrible thing to think that people reverence the national, state, and local governments more than they do God Almighty and His ministers. Let us see to it that we believers hold God's Word in reverence and have no debts to our leaders in the Body of Christ, for they are the higher powers ordained of God to keep order in the Church for the benefit of the entire Body.

Chapter Seven

THE TRANSFER OF LEADERSHIP

On November 22, 1963, the day on which John F. Kennedy was assassinated, some friends and I were out hunting when the news flashed over our radio. We were shocked speechless that our President was dead. All of us were stunned beyond words.

While being pensive over the sudden death of our President, this young man who projected such vitality, I thought about how such shocks and jolting changes have occurred throughout the whole of history. There are many Biblical examples of great leaders emerging in the face of this type of turmoil and adversity. When times were oppressive, men and women rose up who believed the greatness of God's Word and whose lives gave direction to those around them in spite of trying circumstances. Such a man was Joshua to whom the leadership of God's people was transferred upon the death of Moses. Moses himself had risen up to lead God's people during a time of great oppression. He led the children of Israel out of the bondage of Egypt to the boundaries of the Promised Land. For forty years he taught them—he taught them both by his walk with God and by his walk among men.

God and Moses' relationship had developed to the point that they were on the best of terms. They spoke intimately, "face to face" as recorded in Exodus 33:11. Psalms 103:7 says that God "made known his ways unto Moses, his acts unto the children of Israel." While the children of Israel saw the acts of God, God told Moses the whys and the wherefores of His acts, the reasons behind them. During the forty years in which Moses led the children of Israel, God's blessings remained upon them because Moses stood, without faltering, in their behalf. Moses interceded time and again for their mistakes and shortcomings, and God always honored Moses' requests. So long as Moses interceded for Israel, God continued to bless the children of Israel, and great and gracious things happened. Yet one day this human monument, Moses, died.

> Joshua 1:2:
> Moses my servant is dead....

What a tremendous personal vacuum Moses' absence made. After Moses had led the children of Israel for forty years, his death surely was as shocking, if not more so, to them than the shock we Americans experienced when President Kennedy was killed. Imagine what it would have been like had John F. Kennedy single-handedly led our nation for forty years, as Moses had led Israel. Suppose Kennedy had taken us through the extreme hardships and great victories experienced by the children of Israel under Moses. Suppose Kennedy had set our original guidelines of life, as Moses had done in giving the children of Israel the commandments from God. Moses instructed the people, he led the people. And the people knew that it was Moses with whom God communicated and to whom God listened. Suddenly that man who had led the children of Israel for forty long years was dead.

What a tremendous shock this was to the people of Israel when they realized that this man who had led them and put up with their murmurings, bickerings, and insecurities for so many years was now gone. The man who had laid out God's guideline for their lives was dead.

Thus Israel needed a new leader. And God already had a leader singled out for them. It was Joshua, Moses' minister, his assistant and understudy, whom God had called to take up the reins of leadership when Moses was no longer there to lead that nation.

Joshua had worked side by side with Moses, faithfully carrying out responsibilities as Moses directed him. Thus Joshua had been an apprentice, so to speak, to Moses. So once Moses was gone, God, being an orderly God, carried on His communications with Joshua.

> Joshua 1:1 and 2:
> Now after the death of Moses the servant of the Lord it came to pass, that the Lord spake unto Joshua the son of Nun, Moses' minister, saying,
>
> Moses my servant is dead. . . .

God spoke to Joshua, Moses' minister, and said, "Moses my servant is dead." If you could read these words in the original text, you would observe how mournful and hard they are. I can't express these words—"Moses my servant is dead"—to you in English the way they are written in the original. They held all the pathos and all the feeling Joshua would have felt after being associated forty years with the strong, demanding leadership of this one man, Moses.

I have often thought of Joshua and God's call

to him. Would you have wanted to be Joshua that day? No, thanks. Moses had had his hands full leading those stiff-necked Israelites. One day they would sing God's praises, and the next day they would build a golden calf to worship. One day they would say, "Oh, Lord, we'll always do your will." The next day they would conspire to overthrow Moses as their leader. Knowing the Israelites' pattern of behavior, how would you like to have been Joshua when God called him?

Put yourself in the context of this situation. When the Lord spoke to Joshua shortly after Moses' death, the children of Israel were in grief; tears were flowing. But people can't stay in mourning forever. That is why God spoke those weighty words to Joshua that day, saying, "Moses my servant is dead." God was trying to get Joshua and the rest of Israel going by pointing out that they could no longer rely on Moses; Moses was gone. He wasn't going to guide and intercede for Israel ever again. God as much as said to Joshua, "Yes, Moses is dead, but others live on. So get over your mourning and start moving again toward the goal of entering and living in the Promised Land."

Joshua actually had been prepared for this assignment. Leadership was not just suddenly

n out of the blue. One example of
ng was the time that Moses sent
eleven other spies into the Prom-
bring back scouting reports. In
ing out the land, two of the twelve
spies advised Moses to go immediately into the
land and claim it without delay.

> Numbers 14:6-9:
> And Joshua the son of Nun, and Caleb the
> son of Jephunneh, *which were* of them that
> searched the land, rent their clothes:
>
> And they spake unto all the company of the
> children of Israel, saying, The land, which
> we passed through to search it, *is* an ex-
> ceeding good land.
>
> If the Lord delight in us, then he will bring
> us into this land, and give it us; a land which
> floweth with milk and honey.
>
> Only rebel not ye against the Lord, neither
> fear ye the people of the land; for they *are*
> bread for us: their defence is departed from
> them, and the Lord *is* with us: fear them
> not.

Joshua and Caleb showed strong personal
character and confidence in the power of
Jehovah. Not one of the other ten spies advised

Moses to lead the children of Israel into the Promised Land at that time because those ten spies feared the circumstances; they did not trust the strength of God.

As you know, the children of Israel did not enter the land at that time because they sided with the reports of the ten fearful spies, rather than with the believing reports of Joshua and Caleb. But God did reward, as He always does, the believing stand of Joshua and Caleb as they alone of their generation did eventually live in the Promised Land.

Numbers 32:11 and 12:
Surely none of the men that came up out of Egypt, from twenty years old and upward, shall see the land which I sware unto Abraham, unto Isaac, and unto Jacob; because they have not wholly followed me:
Save Caleb the son of Jephunneh the Kenezite, and Joshua the son of Nun: for they have wholly followed the Lord.

Besides being a capable spy, Joshua also served as Israel's commander in battle.

Exodus 17:9-14:
And Moses said unto Joshua, Choose us

113

out men, and go out, fight with Amalek: to morrow I will stand on the top of the hill with the rod of God in mine hand.

So Joshua did as Moses had said to him, and fought with Amalek: and Moses, Aaron, and Hur went up to the top of the hill.

And it came to pass, when Moses held up his hand, that Israel prevailed: and when he let down his hand, Amalek prevailed.

But Moses' hands *were* heavy; and they took a stone, and put *it* under him, and he sat thereon; and Aaron and Hur stayed up his hands, the one on the one side, and the other on the other side; and his hands were steady until the going down of the sun.

And Joshua discomfited Amalek and his people with the edge of the sword.

And the Lord said unto Moses, Write this *for* a memorial in a book, and rehearse *it* in the ears of Joshua: for I will utterly put out the remembrance of Amalek from under heaven.

Moses and Joshua not only worked together in annihilating the Amalekites, but then God told Moses to write down the account of the event and repeat the story for Joshua to hear—to make an even greater impact, a longer lasting impression on Joshua. Moses and Joshua were working together, as we know in retrospect, to prepare Joshua for leadership.

Exodus 24:13:
And Moses rose up, and his minister Joshua....

Joshua was a minister, a helper, an assistant to Moses. He was always devoted and meek to God and to God's servant, Moses.

Exodus 33:11:
And the Lord spake unto Moses face to face, as a man speaketh unto his friend. And he turned again into the camp: but his servant Joshua, the son of Nun, a young man, departed not out of the tabernacle.

Joshua, by his own personal qualities and choice of priorities, was preparing himself in lesser roles of leadership so that God could place him in a greater position of leadership.

The day finally came when Moses was given command by God to proclaim Joshua as Israel's leader, the man who would take charge after Moses' death.

Numbers 27:18-23:

And the Lord said unto Moses, Take thee Joshua the son of Nun, a man in whom *is* the spirit, and lay thine hand upon him;

And set him before Eleazar the priest, and before all the congregation; and give him a charge in their sight.

And thou shalt put *some* of thine honour upon him, that all the congregation of the children of Israel may be obedient.

And he shall stand before Eleazar the priest, who shall ask *counsel* for him after the judgment of Urim before the Lord: at his word shall they go out, and at his word they shall come in, *both* he, and all the children of Israel with him, even all the congregation.

And Moses did as the Lord commanded him: and he took Joshua, and set him before Eleazar the priest, and before all the congregation:

And he laid his hands upon him, and gave him a charge, as the Lord commanded by the hand of Moses.

Thus Joshua was designated by Moses, before his death, and by the high priest as the one to whom "all the congregation of the children of

Israel may [should] be obedient." Joshua was Moses' "heir apparent." He was installed when Moses "laid his hands upon him, and gave him a charge" before all the people as the designated leader.

We have seen how this call to overall leadership was not suddenly thrust upon Joshua. Joshua had been maturing and preparing for that position since his youth when he had helped spy out the Promised Land. So when Moses died, there was no lapse in leadership for the children of Israel. All preparations had been made, and the people understood what God's and Moses' commands were.

> Deuteronomy 34:5-10:
> So Moses the servant of the Lord died there in the land of Moab, according to the word of the Lord.
>
> And he [God] buried him in a valley in the land of Moab, over against Bethpeor: but no man knoweth of his sepulchre unto this day.
>
> And Moses *was* an hundred and twenty years old when he died: his eye was not dim, nor his natural force abated.
>
> And the children of Israel wept for Moses in the plains of Moab thirty days: so the days

of weeping *and* mourning for Moses were ended.

And Joshua the son of Nun was full of the spirit of wisdom; for Moses had laid his hands upon him: and the children of Israel hearkened unto him, and did as the Lord commanded Moses.

And there arose not a prophet since in Israel like unto Moses, whom the Lord knew face to face.

There has been only one prophet in all of history greater than Moses, and that was Jesus Christ himself, the Son of God. Moses was not the Son of God, but he was a man who believed God; thus God gave him tremendous revelation and great light for leadership. In the transferring of leadership, Moses laid his hands on Joshua according to God's command so that Joshua would be "full of the spirit" to receive revelation and light from God.

Deuteronomy 34:9:
And Joshua the son of Nun was full of the spirit of wisdom; for Moses had laid his hands upon him: and the children of Israel hearkened unto him, and did as the Lord commanded Moses.

118

Moses was filled with the spirit. He had the spirit of God upon him, and therefore God was able to speak to him. Moses was able to walk and talk with God. And in the process of his walk, Moses was told by God to lay his hands on Joshua, thus signifying God's presence with Joshua. God was making His provisions for orderly succession of leadership. Thus Joshua, when Moses laid his hands on him, became a man filled with the spirit.

For forty long, laborious years Moses led the stubborn Israelites, and God's Word clearly demonstrates that they were stubborn. Time and time and time again they revolted against the wisdom of Moses and brought problems to themselves. At those times Moses would intercede with God and God would concede Moses' requests. For forty years Moses dealt with the blind-hearted children of Israel; he was the only man who could do so at that time.*

Moses loved God and loved the children of Israel. But Moses wasn't going to live forever. So in preparation for this eventuality, God began

---

*Moses could handle the stiff-necked Israelites because he had a God-given ministry at that time to God's people. And when a person has a ministry of service to God's people, he or she can tolerate a lot of things that he or she never could otherwise.

training Joshua for leadership many years before Moses' death. However, even with all that training under Moses, Joshua still must have been greatly challenged by the call to take charge after Moses' death. But because Joshua was meek, he attended to God's commands and overcame any insecurities he may have had. He was stunned when Moses died, but God commanded him to take the lead.

> Joshua 1:1 and 2:
> Now after the death of Moses the servant of the Lord it came to pass, that the Lord spake unto Joshua the son of Nun, Moses' minister, saying,
>
> Moses my servant is dead; now therefore arise, go over this Jordan, thou, and all this people, unto the land which I do give to them, *even* to the children of Israel.

The essence of what God told Joshua that day was, "Joshua, now you're in charge. So take charge and move! Don't wait a while, but go into the Promised Land now." Joshua could have cowered and backed off, saying, "Oh, no, the river's at flood stage. Besides, directly on the other side waits the enemy, and that enemy is the best-equipped army in the whole world. They've got massive weaponry, even nuclear power.''

But God didn't have a discussion with Joshua. God simply gave the command, ''Now therefore arise, go over this Jordan.'' Joshua was to have the children of Israel pack up and begin moving immediately.

> Joshua 1:10 and 11:
> Then Joshua commanded the officers of the people, saying,
> Pass through the host, and command the people, saying, Prepare you victuals; for within three days ye shall pass over this Jordan, to go in to possess the land, which the Lord your God giveth you to possess it.

God said to Joshua, in verse 2, ''You get the people ready and walk them into the land that I am giving you.'' Well, if God gives something, who do you think is going to take it away? If God said to march into the Promised Land, then those who obeyed were going to be landholders. Who do you think was going to stop them? I tell you, even the most precisely aimed artillery couldn't have hit one of them.

121

No matter how great the enemy, no matter what the obstacle, when God has given the command to go, you must move. So long as you and I live according to the greatness of God's Word, all the enemies and all the obstacles of the world can't stop us because God's Word is powerful and effective and it lasts forever!

The Word of the Lord came and Joshua was able to take over when Moses' life ended. From a senses point of view, it would seem impossible to step into the position just held by Moses. But God always has and always will make available the power, the knowledge, and the ability to carry out a given responsibility.

God told Joshua to arise. He didn't tell him to sit and mourn for another six months to lament the fact that Moses was dead. Whenever a person—including a man of God—dies, life for the living doesn't stop. The things of God must go on; therefore, the message would be the same today as it was to Joshua, "Arise, get on the move, and overcome whatever hurdle there is in front of you."

Originally, when Moses had brought Israel out of Egypt, God had planned for them to march directly into the Promised Land and to inhabit it.

But because of unbelief, sin, and general short-comings, God never instructed Moses to take them into the land of their inheritance. Even Moses himself was not permitted to enter. But now the time was right, and God said to Joshua, "Joshua, get up. Quit stewing and fretting because my great servant Moses is gone. You must now assume the leadership. So arise and go over the Jordan." And God didn't stop there. He gave Joshua some tremendous encouragement.

> Joshua 1:3:
> Every place that the sole of your foot shall tread upon, that have I given [past tense] unto you, as I said unto Moses.

God put in the past tense what was yet to come to pass. The children of Israel needed only to arise and go. God said, "Every place that the sole of your foot shall tread upon, that have I [already] given unto you."

Notice that God said, "I've already given it." God repeated for Joshua the promise He had made to Moses and to the children of Israel in Deuteronomy 11:24. The God Who created the heavens and the earth is not going to let a little thing like the Jordan River stop Him from moving forward. Nor will the enemies on the other side of that river stop Him. The word was "Arise and go."

Many people might hesitate after this clipped command and say, "Lord, your Word is wonderful, but I've got to think this through. Maybe I'll be ready tomorrow; or maybe the next day. I don't know if I'm up to it right now." When God gives you specific instructions, He expects you to take action. He doesn't expect you to procrastinate. We could die by hesitating to act on God's Word. But, if we dare to rise now with the greatness of God's Word and hold forth that greatness, God will again conquer the enemy and we will again victoriously cross the rivers of life—even at flood stage.

It's a remarkable thing that God put His promise in the past tense—"I have already given to you"—and He still does this today. Many, many times He puts in the past tense what still is the future for us. Things that God has promised us in His Word are already God's will for us if we'll only arise and cross our personal Jordans. But most people hesitate to arise; they're afraid of the obstacles with which they're confronted, the problems which they encounter. They are put off by circumstances rather than relying on God's Word. But not so Joshua.

124

Joshua 1:4:
From the wilderness and this Lebanon even unto the great river, the river Euphrates, all the land of the Hittites, and unto the great sea toward the going down of the sun, shall be your coast.

God specifically named and described the boundaries of the land that He had already designated for the children of Israel.

Verse 5:
There shall not any man [women too, because it's an inclusive noun] be able to stand before [against, as to obstruct] thee all the days of thy life....

God promised Joshua that there would be no person able to stand against him all the days of his life. What comfort and encouragement this revelation must have been to the heart of Joshua. Perhaps Joshua was reflecting on the great man, Moses. So God said to Joshua, "Why are you looking at Moses? I want to tell you there's not going to be a man able to stand before you." There would not be anybody who would have the ability to confront Joshua and outdo him in any way, shape, or form.

What reassurance this must have been to Joshua who had stepped into the position of the monumental Moses. To have God say to him, "There shall not any man be able to stand against thee all the days of thy life" has to be encouragement of the strongest kind.

> ...as I was with Moses, *so* I [God] will be with thee: I will not fail thee, nor forsake thee.

"...I will not fail thee, nor forsake thee." Has God changed? The same God that was with Moses and Joshua is the same God Who is with us today. Isn't it wonderful to know that God is with you, that He will not fail you, that He will not forsake you? The same God Who met Joshua's needs meets our needs. And therefore, He is saying to us, "Arise, start moving."

What dynamic believing these assurances from God made possible. God said, "Joshua, I'll be with you just as I was with Moses. I did not fail him, and I won't fail or forsake you either. So now arise, go over the Jordan."

To go over Jordan at the moment God spoke to Joshua held a slight complication from a physical aspect: the Jordan was at flood stage. The scripture says that the river was out of its

126

banks. But this was no problem for God. God said to Joshua, "Tell the priests to put the ark on their shoulders and start walking." And that's what Joshua did.

> Joshua 3:6-8:
> And Joshua spake unto the priests, saying, Take up the ark of the covenant, and pass over before the people. And they took up the ark of the covenant, and went before the people.
>
> And the Lord said unto Joshua, This day will I begin to magnify thee [Joshua] in the sight of all Israel, that they may know that, as I was with Moses, *so* I will be with thee.
>
> And thou shalt command the priests that bear the ark of the covenant, saying, When ye are come to the brink of the water of Jordan, ye shall stand still in Jordan.

Now just imagine those orders. Flood stage. Do you know what the average person would have done? Argued awhile: "But, Lord, the river is at flood stage. Lord, why not wait until the water goes down? Or maybe we should make a few rafts? Give us a few motorboats and amphibious equipment." But the Lord said to Joshua, "Walk!" So Joshua gathered the priests, and he commanded them, "Walk." The scripture says that as the feet of the priests who carried the ark of the covenant touched the edge of the water, the waters began to recede. That's walking according to God's revealed Word.

> Joshua 3:15 and 16:
> And as they that bare the ark were come unto Jordan, and the feet of the priests that bare the ark were dipped in the brim of the water, (for Jordan overfloweth all his banks all the time of harvest,)
>
> That the waters which came down from above stood *and* rose up upon an heap very far from the city Adam, that *is* beside Zaretan: and those that came down toward the sea of the plain, *even* the salt sea, failed, *and* were cut off: and the people passed over right against Jericho.

When Joshua was given God's Word, he immediately carried through on it. And what results! When the average person today gets the Word of God, he wants to argue about it. The Word of the Lord is always clear, it's always plain, and God can't do a thing for you or me until we take action. God said, "Walk across the Jordan, even at flood stage." Is it any harder for

God to move a flood out of the way than to move fifteen drops of water? He stopped the waters of the Red Sea in a wall for Moses. Would He do less for Joshua? Same God, same power, same promise. "...As I was with Moses, *so* I will be with thee...." What tremendous believing those men had!

> Joshua 1:6:
> Be strong and of a good courage: for unto this people shalt thou divide for an inheritance the land, which I sware unto their fathers to give them.

"Be strong...." Strong in whom? The Lord. We can't be strong in our own strength. Our poor strength, what little there is, lasts only a few earthly years. You and I have to be strong in the strength of the Lord. When we are strong in the Lord, we will have good courage. Why should we fear since God in Christ has conquered fear for us? Why should we be discouraged when He has conquered discouragement? Why should we be downcast when He has conquered every reason for being downcast?

Discouragement is always from the Devil. Whenever we get discouraged, we are always wrong. Our God made us more than conquerors through Jesus Christ who loved us and gave himself for us.

God said to Joshua, "Be strong and of a good courage: for unto this people shalt thou [Joshua] divide for an inheritance the land, which I sware unto their fathers to give them." Long before this, God had promised the land to Abraham, the forefather of these people. Now God had brought the children of Abraham back to this land to inherit it.

> Verse 7:
> Only be thou strong and very courageous, that thou mayest observe to do according to all the law, which Moses my servant commanded thee: turn not from it *to* the right hand or *to* the left, that thou mayest prosper [*sakal*] whithersoever thou goest.

Only be strong and very courageous. For the second time, the Word of the Lord to Joshua is to be strong, stand faithful, stay put, be courageous. God not only told Joshua once; He told him twice.

We, too, have to keep telling ourselves, repeating to ourselves, the same thing: Be strong in the Word of the Lord and be very courageous in walking on the Word of God. For it's only as we

130

arise and start walking that the obstacles with which we are confronted will ever be overcome. So long as we sit looking at them in a slump of discouragement, we will always be overcome by the presence of the obstacles. But as we start walking and approach the situation with believing, the obstacles begin to dissolve. Moving ahead in the face of obstacles takes believing and trusting God.

God reminded Joshua to "observe to do according to all the law, which Moses my servant commanded thee." In other words, "Don't turn to the right or to the left, but stay unswervingly on God's Word." You see, the law was the Word of God to Joshua as well as to Moses. And if you have the Word of God, you know what God's will is. Then you had better not turn to the right or to the left. Just carry it out, right to the letter. The Word of God is the will of God. It means what it says and says what it means. If you stay faithful to your calling, God says that you will prosper wherever you go.

"...That thou mayest prosper whithersoever thou goest." The word "prosper," *sakal* in Hebrew, is elsewhere translated "to act wisely" or "understand." You will act with wisdom and have understanding at all times when you adhere to God's Word.

131

After giving Joshua this encouragement, God then told Joshua to continue speaking and to constantly meditate on His Word.

> Verse 8:
> This book of the law [the Word of God] shall not depart out of thy mouth; but thou shalt meditate therein day and night....

God said, "You don't need to run around all day gossiping or telling dirty stories. If you're going to use your mouth, you should speak God's Word." That's what God says here in Joshua 1:8: "This book of the law shall not depart out of thy mouth...." When you talk, you talk God's truth.

God also instructed Joshua to meditate in that law day and night—in other words, all the time, constantly. He didn't tell him to immerse himself in newspapers and periodicals, radio and televison programs. He didn't tell him to meditate on a theologian's teaching. God said to Joshua, "Speak this law and meditate on it. Make this Word the center of your life day and night."

You have to put the Word of God in your life so that whenever you speak, it is the Word being spoken, it is truth being spoken. Don't let it depart out of your mouth and meditate in it day

132

and night. Keep speaking God's Word, keep thinking God's Word, and align your thinking and living with it.

> ...that thou mayest observe to do according to all that is written therein: for then thou shalt make thy way prosperous, and then thou shalt have good success.

God told Joshua that if he observed and lived according to the law of the Lord, then Joshua would be prosperous and have good success. When we do the will of God, we too prosper and succeed. And certainly we should prosper, shouldn't we? God expects us to prosper.

> III John 2:
> Beloved, I wish above all things that thou mayest prosper....

How do we as believers become prosperous? By putting God's Word at the center of our lives as our rule book of believing and practice. The Word of God gives us the rules whereby God's spiritual ball game is played. His rules must be adhered to. We can't make up new rules as we go along. Prosperity—in all its forms—is dependent upon our believing God's Word and continuing in it.

The key to sustained prosperity and success is to remain faithful to God's Word. We see this principle throughout the life of Joshua. God exhorted Joshua a third time to be strong and courageous.

> Joshua 1:9:
> Have not I commanded thee? Be strong and of a good courage; be not afraid, neither be thou dismayed....

God told Joshua in verse 6, in verse 7, and now again in verse 9 to be strong and courageous. The first thing the enemy always endeavors to do is to introduce fear into our lives. But when we're strong and of good courage, what happens to the fear? It's dispelled; it's gone. So Satan can't even get a toehold in our lives if we're strong and of good courage. "...Be not afraid, neither be thou dismayed...." Do not be downcast by anything. Why? "...For the Lord thy God *is* with thee...."

That is why Joshua could rise up and move ahead with the leadership of God's people upon Moses' death. And that's the greatest thing to know in the world today—that the Lord your God is with you. To know that you're a Christian, born again of God's Spirit, filled with the holy spirit, is the greatest truth you have in your life today. To know that you're heaven bound in the midst of all the hubbub of society and the involvements of the world in which you live. With God in Christ in you, the hope of glory, with eternal life, why should you ever be afraid? "...Be not afraid...." Be not afraid and you will not be dismayed. Why?

> ...for the Lord thy God *is* with thee whithersoever thou goest.

Wherever we go, we can be energized and can overflow with the greatness of the power of God. Our God is with us wherever we are. God protects us, He keeps us, He inspires us, He guides us, He takes care of us.

To know that you know that you know that the Lord your God is with you is the greatest message to the heart of any man or woman. If the servants of God in the Old Testament were able to believe God's Word and follow His instructions with such obedience, don't you think that you and I who are born again of God's Spirit could follow God's instructions and manifest His peace and prosperity? Surely, the Lord our God is with us.

135

Verse 9:

...Be strong and of a good courage; be not afraid, neither be thou dismayed: for the Lord thy God *is* with thee whithersoever thou goest.

Men and women come and go—are born, live, and die—as did Moses and Joshua. But the God of Moses and Joshua, Who caused them to prosper in some extremely difficult circumstances, is our God today. God is with you; God is by your side; God lives within you. So move with the greatness of His Word, trusting that Word to the last letter. Now is the time. Arise, go, move onward to hold forth God's Word, "for then thou shalt make thy way prosperous, and then thou shalt have good success." *God* has promised it. *You* believe it. And *you* shall see God's magnificent success in your life.

PART III

GOD'S ORDER
IN
OLD TESTAMENT
TIMES

PART III

GOD'S ORDER IN OLD TESTAMENT TIMES

Through the centuries, men and women have come and gone, but God's Word lives and will continue to abide forever. The accounts of Old Testament believers to whom God revealed Himself are written for our learning. In this part of *Order My Steps in Thy Word,* God's order in the lives of three individual believers from the Old Testament is studied.

"A Man in Whom the Spirit of God Is" gives the record of Joseph's deliverance from prison in Egypt and his rise to responsibility in Pharaoh's kingdom. It was Pharaoh who made the observation that no one was so wise and discreet as Joseph, "a man in whom the Spirit of God *is.*" Because Joseph ordered his steps according to God's Word, he and all Egypt, as well as the children of Israel, were not only delivered from potential destruction, but they were able to prosper.

The chapter entitled "Choose You This Day" shows God's man Joshua challenging the children of Israel to put away their idolatrous practices and commit their ways to Jehovah even after Joshua's death.

"The Way of Life or Death" offers the two choices that face all mankind. This chapter illustrates the choices as heralded by the Prophet Jeremiah to people who chose *not* to have God order their steps and who thus suffered the consequences.

Chapter Eight

A MAN IN WHOM THE SPIRIT OF GOD IS

There is a record in the Old Testament of a man whose stand for God gave rise to the greatest nation in the world at that time. The man was Joseph. The nation was Egypt. What was it that Joseph did to bring ancient Egypt to such great prominence? He listened to God, and then he faithfully carried out His instructions. These two keys—listening and carrying out—are foundational to the success of any person or any family or any nation.

When I first began to understand the record of Joseph in chapters 37 through 41 of Genesis, I walked on air for days. Seeing how God moved in the life of one human being was electrifying. Very few people throughout history have learned to listen to God as Joseph did; even fewer have learned to walk in obedience. For Joseph, the Word of God was the will of God.

According to Genesis 37, Joseph went to Egypt

under adverse circumstances. His brothers intensely disliked him. They were jealous of Joseph because their father, Jacob, had given him the robe of heirship.* The brothers were further antagonized by Joseph when he told them about his dreams that pictured his ruling over them. Joseph's brothers considered slaying him, but his oldest brother Reuben ruled out that idea. So the brothers compromised by selling Joseph into slavery. Joseph's owners took him to Egypt where he was resold and eventually unjustly thrown into prison. In the midst of all these deplorable events in Joseph's life, God was making provisions for the salvaging of a whole nation, Israel. Obviously Egypt also benefited from God's plan as Egypt became one of the strongest, most enduring civilizations of all time. But the ultimate purpose of Egypt's prosperity was for God to keep His promise to Abraham—to raise up a great nation from Abraham's offspring, the children of Israel.

In this chapter, I want to focus on Joseph and his influence on the nation of Egypt. Let's take

*The "coat of *many* colours" of Genesis 37:3 was a garment given only to the man chosen as heir. Thus, Joseph's brothers were jealous because their father, Jacob, had chosen their *younger* brother as his heir. Barbara M. Bowen, *Strange Scriptures That Perplex the Western Mind* (Grand Rapids: Wm. B. Eerdmans, 1944), pp. 43,44.

up the account of Joseph in the thirty-ninth chapter of Genesis when Joseph was in prison as a virtual nobody.

> Genesis 39:20 and 21:
> And Joseph's master took him, and put him into the prison, a place where the king's prisoners *were* bound: and he was there in the prison.
> But the Lord was with Joseph [even in prison], and shewed him mercy, and gave him favour in the sight of the keeper [warden] of the prison.

Joseph was in a maximum security prison, incarcerated with the king's prisoners. But the Lord was with Joseph and showed him mercy and gave him favor, putting him in the good graces of the keeper of the prison, the warden.

> Verse 22:
> And the keeper of the prison committed to Joseph's hand all the prisoners that *were* in the prison; and whatsoever they did there, he was the doer *of it*.

These responsibilities weren't given to Joseph immediately after he was put in prison. It took time for Joseph to demonstrate to the warden his fine character and abilities and to gain the warden's confidence.

Verse 23:
The keeper of the prison looked not to any thing *that was* under his [Joseph's] hand; because the Lord was with him, and *that* which he did, the Lord made *it* to prosper.

Who made Joseph's deeds to prosper? The Lord. You see, you've got to believe that God is going to cause you to prosper, no matter where you are. In a prison, a person cannot do very much on his own. But even there, if a believer just does his part with integrity, then the Lord can make the circumstances profitable. A believer can prosper even in that environment.

Genesis 40:1-8:
And it came to pass after these things, *that* the butler of the king of Egypt and *his* baker had offended their lord the king of Egypt.

And Pharaoh was wroth [very angry] against two *of* his officers, against the chief of the butlers, and against the chief of the bakers.

And he put them in ward [in prison] in the house of the captain of the guard, into the prison, the place where Joseph *was* bound [confined].

And the captain of the guard charged Joseph with them, and he served them: and they continued a season in ward.

And they dreamed a dream both of them [the butler and the baker], each man his dream in one night, each man according to the interpretation of his dream, the butler and the baker of the king of Egypt, which *were* bound [confined] in the prison.

And Joseph came in unto them in the morning, and looked upon them, and, behold, they *were* sad.

And he asked Pharaoh's officers that *were* with him in the ward of his lord's house, saying, Wherefore look ye *so* sadly to day?

And they said unto him, We have dreamed a dream, and *there is* no interpreter of it. [Nobody is able to tell us what our dreams mean.] And Joseph said unto them, *Do* not interpretations *belong* to God? tell me *them,* I pray you.

What tremendous instruction for us. Many times we are at a loss to fully understand a situation. Our own sense knowledge can only take us

145

so far. But revelation from God can give us an awareness and an understanding of things unseen. Just as the unfolding of His Word belongs to God, so truly the interpretation of the dreams belonged to God.

> Verses 9-11:
> And the chief butler told his dream to Joseph, and said to him, In my dream, behold, a vine *was* before me;
>
> And in the vine *were* three branches: and it *was* as though it budded, *and* her blossoms shot forth; and the clusters thereof brought forth ripe grapes:
>
> And Pharaoh's cup *was* in my hand: and I took the grapes, and pressed them into Pharaoh's cup, and I gave the cup into Pharaoh's hand.

Verses 9, 10, and 11 describe the butler's dream. Now we must ask ourselves the question: What was the significance of the vine with the three branches? By conjecture, it could have meant any number of things. Joseph could have used his own private interpretation to make the dream mean anything he desired. But Joseph knew that the interpretations belonged to God. What

146

cannot be known by the five senses can be known and understood when God gives revelation.

Verse 12:
And Joseph said unto him, This *is* the interpretation of it: The three branches *are* three days.

Joseph could not have known this by his own senses; he needed revelation. God revealed the dream's interpretation to him, because he could not know it by his own observation or knowledge.

Verse 13:
Yet within three days shall Pharaoh lift up thine head, and restore thee unto thy place: and thou shalt deliver Pharaoh's cup into his hand, after the former manner when thou wast his butler.

This was good news for the butler. Joseph said that he would be restored to his former position within three days. Knowing this, Joseph made a request of the butler.

Verses 14 and 15:
But think on me [Joseph] when it shall be

147

well with thee, and shew kindness, I pray
thee, unto me, and make mention of me unto
Pharaoh, and bring me out of this house:

For indeed I was stolen away out of the land
of the Hebrews: and here also have I done
nothing that they should put me into the
dungeon.

Joseph also received revelation to tell the
butler to mention him to Pharaoh. After speaking to the butler, Joseph next interpreted the
baker's dream.

Verses 16-19:
When the chief baker saw that the interpretation was good, he said unto Joseph, I
also *was* in my dream, and, behold, *I had*
three white baskets on my head:

And in the uppermost basket *there was* of all
manner of bakemeats for Pharaoh; and the
birds did eat them out of the basket upon
my head.

And Joseph answered and said, This *is* the
interpretation thereof: The three baskets *are*
three days:

Yet within three days shall Pharaoh lift up
thy head from off thee, and shall hang thee

on a tree; and the birds shall eat thy flesh from off thee.

The baker was expecting a similar interpretation of encouragement such as Joseph had spoken to the butler. But the revelation was far from what the baker anticipated. The interpretation of the dream was that within three days the baker would be hanged. The account in Genesis 40 continues, showing how the interpretations of the two dreams were fulfilled.

> Verses 20-22:
> And it came to pass the third day, *which was* Pharaoh's birthday, that he made a feast unto all his servants: and he lifted up the head of the chief butler and of the chief baker among his servants.
>
> And he restored the chief butler unto his butlership again; and he gave the cup into Pharaoh's hand:
>
> But he hanged the chief baker: as Joseph had interpreted to them.

And then the next verse is so truly human. So often we forget the people who have blessed our lives.

Verse 23:
Yet did not the chief butler remember
Joseph, but forgat him.

So it is with most people, even the best of us.
The adversary wants us to forget our benefac-
tors. The butler could have gone to Pharaoh and
said, ''A most unusual thing happened while I
was in prison.'' And then he could have told
Pharaoh how Joseph had interpreted both his
and the baker's dreams, and how the interpretations came to pass even as Joseph had said. But
the butler did not do that; he became caught up
in the routine activities of life and forgot about
Joseph.

Genesis 41:1:
And it came to pass at the end of two full
years. . . .

This forty-first chapter begins two years after
the events of chapter 40. How long Joseph was in
jail before this we do not know. But we do know
that two years after the butler's release, Pharaoh
had some troubling dreams.

Verses 1-4:
And it came to pass at the end of two full

years, that Pharaoh dreamed: and, behold, he stood by the river.

And, behold, there came up out of the river seven well favoured kine [cattle] and fatfleshed [meaty cattle]; and they fed in a meadow [plenty to eat].

And, behold, seven other kine [cattle] came up after them out of the river, ill favoured and leanfleshed [skin and bones]; and [they] stood by the *other* kine [cattle] upon the brink of the river.

And the ill favoured and leanfleshed kine did eat up the seven well favoured and fat kine. So Pharaoh awoke.

Normally, cattle are not cannibalistic—they do not eat each other. So Pharaoh was sure this dream had a meaning, but what could it be?

Verses 5-9:
And he [Pharaoh] slept and dreamed the second time: and, behold, seven ears of corn came up upon one stalk, rank and good.

And, behold, seven thin ears and blasted with the east wind sprung up after them.

And the seven thin ears devoured the seven rank and full ears. And Pharaoh awoke, and, behold, *it was* a dream.

151

And it came to pass in the morning that his spirit was troubled [Pharaoh was disturbed]; and he sent and called for all the magicians [all the spiritualists] of Egypt, and all the wise men thereof: and Pharaoh told them his dream; but *there was* none that could interpret them unto Pharaoh.

Then spake the chief butler unto Pharaoh, saying, I do remember my faults this day.

After Pharaoh had searched all Egypt for someone to interpret his dreams and all had failed to interpret them, the butler remembered Joseph, the accurate interpreter of both his dream and the baker's dream. At long last the butler recalled his promise to mention Joseph to Pharaoh. It was two full years before his memory was jolted. Thus, the butler approached Pharaoh to tell him of Joseph.

Verses 10-13:
[The butler recalled] Pharaoh was wroth with his servants, and put me in ward in the captain of the guard's house, *both* me and the chief baker:

And we dreamed a dream in one night, I and he; we dreamed each man according to the interpretation of his dream.

And *there was* there with us a young man, an Hebrew, servant to the captain of the guard; and we told him, and he interpreted to us our dreams; to each man according to his dream he did interpret.

And it came to pass, as he interpreted to us, so it was; me he restored unto mine office, and him he hanged.

After two full years the butler remembered and acted on Joseph's simple request to "think on me" and "make mention of me unto Pharaoh." At this point, events in Joseph's life began to accelerate.

Verse 14:
Then Pharaoh sent and called Joseph, and they brought him hastily out of the dungeon: and he shaved *himself,* and changed his raiment, and came in unto Pharaoh.

Before Joseph appeared before Pharaoh, he cleaned up and changed his clothes to meet the king appropriately groomed. In representing God, we, too, should put our best foot forward and be as attractive as we can be. Now, clothes don't make the person, but they surely help the impression one person makes on another. What

153

people have in their hearts is most important; but, still, as ambassadors for God, we should dress as is fitting for God's representatives.

Joseph shaved himself and changed his garment before he was brought before Pharaoh. And yet God's Word says they brought him "hastily out of the dungeon." These little details simply delight me. That God would take time in His Word to tell us that Joseph shaved lets us see that people in the Bible were as human as we are. Why should God's Word include details like that? Simply to teach us about the greatness of God and the real, breathing people who walked in that greatness. It encourages us to walk with God. And, I want to tell you, Joseph was definitely walking.

> Verse 15:
> And Pharaoh said unto Joseph, I have dreamed a dream, and *there is* none that can interpret it: and I have heard say of thee, *that* thou canst understand a dream to interpret it.

Now, this was quite a position for Joseph to be in. He could have put real leverage on Pharaoh, saying, "I can do it, Pharaoh, but first tell me what it's worth to you. What are you going to do for me in return for my interpreting your dream?'' But he didn't. Joseph walked by the power of God; he trusted God to work in the situation. God was Joseph's sufficiency, not Pharaoh. And indeed God took care of Joseph in a way that Joseph could never have done by his own power.

> Verse 16:
> And Joseph answered Pharaoh, saying, *It is* not in me: God shall give Pharaoh an answer of peace.

The first point Joseph made to Pharaoh was that the interpretation was from God and not from him. And then he immediately proceeded to comfort Pharaoh with the revelation that the interpretation would be an answer of peace.

> Verse 17:
> And Pharaoh said unto Joseph, In my dream...

Then Pharaoh told Joseph his dream. Remember the seven fat cattle and the seven lean ones, and the seven good ears of corn and the seven thin ones? The lean cattle devoured the fat cattle and the thin ears of corn devoured the full ears. All this Pharaoh told Joseph.

155

Verse 25:
And Joseph said unto Pharaoh, The dream
[the two dreams] of Pharaoh *is* one: God
hath shewed Pharaoh what he *is* about to
do.

How did Joseph know this? God was revealing
it to him.

Verse 26:
The seven good kine [cattle] *are* seven
years....

We by our senses could not know what the
seven cattle and seven ears of corn stood for any
more than we could know what the three vines
and the three baskets in the earlier dreams stood
for. In Pharaoh's dream seven represented the
number of years.

Verses 26-32:
The seven good kine [cattle] *are* seven years;
and the seven good ears *are* seven years: the
dream *is* one.

And the seven thin and ill favoured kine
[cattle] that came up after them *are* seven
years; and the seven empty ears blasted with
the east wind shall be seven years of famine.

This *is* the thing which I have spoken unto Pharaoh: What God *is* about to do he sheweth unto Pharaoh.

Behold, there come seven years of great plenty throughout all the land of Egypt:

And there shall arise after them seven years of famine; and all the plenty shall be forgotten in the land of Egypt; and the famine shall consume the land;

And the plenty shall not be known in the land by reason of that famine following; for it *shall be* very grievous.

And for that the dream was doubled unto Pharaoh twice; *it is* because the thing *is* established by God, and God will shortly [immediately] bring it to pass.

What a great revelation! The interpretation ends by saying that because the dream was doubled, dreamed twice, the events it foretold were established and would quickly come to pass. When revelation is given twice, absolutely nothing can change the course of events, for it is established. All the prayers in the world won't change it. When revelation is doubled, it will never change and will occur soon.*

---

*See Deuteronomy 17:6; 19:15; Matthew 18:16; John 8:17; Acts 10:9-18; and II Corinthians 13:1.

157

After Joseph had told Pharaoh about the events which would occur in Egypt for the next fourteen years, what did Pharaoh do? How did he prepare? What would our President give to know what will happen in this country for the next fourteen years? What would he give to know even for his tenure in office?

Suppose you were Pharaoh and you knew that the next seven years would be years of great plenty and the following seven years would be years of devastating famine. What would you, as Pharaoh, do about it? Would you change any of your policies? Would you cut exports? How would this affect your imports? Would you appoint a new Secretary of Agriculture? How much of your harvest would you store for the famine? How would you store it? How much loss would you allow for the mice to eat?

Once Joseph, by revelation, gave Pharaoh the interpretation of his dream, Pharaoh could either accept what Joseph revealed or he could reject it. If he accepted it, he had to decide what actions to take. It is one thing to have knowledge; it is another thing to have the wisdom to act on that knowledge in the best manner. Pharaoh could either rely on his own sense knowledge to determine what he should do in preparing for the next fourteen years, or he could seek God's counsel in dealing with the situation.

The Word of God has much to say about government and governmental leaders. It has much to say on how a nation can best function economically, politically, judicially, and in many other categories. If a nation is to prosper and not be driven to depression, chaos, or weakness, it must ultimately come to God's Word and the principles of that Word. In this situation in Egypt, it was Joseph who was receiving the Word of God. And Joseph continued speaking to Pharaoh after the dream was interpreted, telling him God's plan for the salvation of Egypt during the seven years of great famine, which were yet seven years away.

Verse 33:
Now therefore let Pharaoh look out a man [a single man, not a committee] discreet and wise, and set him over the land of Egypt.

The person Pharaoh appointed to this position of overseeing Egypt was going to be given tremendous responsibility. That person would also be given great authority. Responsibility is impossible to carry out unless authority is given to execute the responsibility. Now if Pharaoh

159

was going to get the results of the Word of God, he had to believe that Joseph was speaking God's Word. Yet Joseph had been in prison. Can a jailbird be trusted? Well, somebody trusted someone, as we are going to see.

> Verse 34:
> Let Pharaoh do *this,* and let him [the man of verse 33] appoint officers [overseers] over the land, and take up the fifth part of the land of Egypt in the seven plenteous years.

Joseph told Pharaoh to appoint a wise man over the land of Egypt. Then this man should appoint officers, or overseers, to collect a fifth part of Egypt's harvest for the next seven years. A fifth part is twenty percent. Joseph said they were to take up only twenty percent of the plenteous harvests and store that. What happened to the other eighty percent in those seven years of plenty? It could have been consumed in Egypt and also traded with other nations. Eighty percent of the harvest during the years of great plenty gave Pharaoh an abundance to work with. Eighty percent of harvest during great plenty was, no doubt, more than one hundred percent of harvest during a normal year.

Verses 35 and 36:
And let them [the overseers] gather all the food of those good years that come, and lay up corn under the hand of Pharaoh, and let them keep food in the cities.

And that food shall be for store to the land against the seven years of famine, which shall be in the land of Egypt; that the land perish not through the famine.

So now we already know that there is not going to be anything left of the food when the seven years of famine are over, because all will have been consumed. Remember, the lean cattle devoured the fat ones, and the lean ears devoured the full ones. And the interpretation was "the plenty shall not be known in the land by reason of that famine following." The stored food would all be gone at the end of the seven years of famine. However, there's certainly no need for leftovers when a famine is over.

Verse 37:
And the thing [Joseph's plan] was good in the eyes of Pharaoh, and in the eyes of all his servants.

Pharaoh's judgment was good; he liked the

plan which Joseph, by revelation from God, had given. Of course, the servants agreed. If Pharaoh said, "I like it," what could the servants say? They had better agree.

> Verse 38:
> And Pharaoh said unto his servants, Can we find *such a one* as this *is,* a man in whom the Spirit of God *is*?

That was a great statement for a leader of Pharaoh's stature to make. This great Pharaoh of Egypt recognized that Joseph was "a man in whom the Spirit of God *is.*" He knew of no other man in the nation who had that spirit of God. This was quite an observation and a declaration to come from Pharoah.

> Verses 39-42:
> And Pharaoh said unto Joseph, Forasmuch as God hath shewed thee all this, *there is* none so discreet and wise as thou *art:*
>
> Thou shalt be over my house, and according unto thy word shall all my people be ruled: only in the throne will I be greater than thou.
>
> And Pharaoh said unto Joseph, See, I have set thee over all the land of Egypt.

And Pharaoh took off his [signet] ring from his hand, and put it upon Joseph's hand...

Joseph was elevated to the position of steward over all the land of Egypt. The authority for this stewardship was the signet ring Pharaoh put upon Joseph's hand.*

...and [Pharaoh] arrayed him [Joseph] in vestures of fine linen, and put a gold chain about his neck.

The gold chain in Egyptian culture stood for honor.

Verse 43:
And he [Pharaoh] made him [Joseph] to ride in the second chariot which he [Pharaoh] had; and they cried before him,

---

*The signet ring given to Joseph was a ring with Pharaoh's seal on it. Joseph then had the same authority as Pharaoh's written signature. For further information about the importance of seals, see J.D. Douglas, ed., *The New Bible Dictionary* (Grand Rapids: Wm. B. Eerdmans, 1962), s.v. "seal, sealing."

When we understand the significance of "sealing," we can begin to appreciate the truth that we as believers have God's seal or signet impression upon us. See Ephesians 1:13.

163

Bow the knee: and he made him *ruler* over all the land of Egypt.

Because the Egyptians bowed their knees, did they believe Joseph was God? No. It simply meant that the people honored Joseph as a man of authority, worthy of great respect.

Verse 44:
And Pharaoh said unto Joseph, I *am* Pharaoh, and without thee shall no man lift up his hand or foot in all the land of Egypt.

I want to tell you, Joseph was given real authority. If Joseph said, "Let that fellow out of jail," what do you think happened? Nobody questioned Joseph's authority. He had the absolute right of control. Joseph was given complete charge, accountable only to Pharaoh.

Joseph had not been thoroughly trained for his job by experience, but he had been trained for it by walking according to God's instructions and by the spirit of God upon him. Education is important, but only leaders walking with the spirit of God can lead a nation out of darkness and chaos. Joseph not only had the spirit of God upon him, but he was also upright and honest.

These should be the greatest qualifications for anyone desiring public office or authority.

> Verse 45:
> And Pharaoh called Joseph's name Zaphnathpaaneah [What a name! It means "revealer of secrets."]; and he gave him to wife Asenath the daughter of Potipherah priest of On. And Joseph went out over *all* the land of Egypt.

Pharaoh didn't ask Joseph if he wanted to marry the priest's daughter. He just said, "Here's a wife for you."

> Verse 46:
> And Joseph *was* thirty years old when he stood before Pharaoh king of Egypt. . . .

Joseph showed a lot of wisdom for a relatively young man. But Joseph's greatness was not just his acuteness of mind; it was his faithfulness in continuing to walk with God. Even when sold into slavery by his brothers and even when living in an Egyptian prison, Joseph was steadfast, having confidence in God and listening to Him. He had the spirit of God upon him.

...And Joseph went out from the presence of Pharaoh, and went throughout all the land of Egypt.

Joseph did not interpret Pharaoh's dream, marry the priest's daughter, and travel throughout Egypt all in one day. This all took place over a period of time.

Verses 47-50:
And in the seven plenteous years the earth brought forth by handfuls.

And he gathered up all the food of the seven years, which were in the land of Egypt, and laid up the food in the cities: the food of the field, which *was* round about every city, laid he up in the same.

And Joseph gathered corn as the sand of the sea, very much, until he left numbering; for *it was* without number.

And unto Joseph were born two sons before the years of famine came, which Asenath the daughter of Potipherah priest of On bare unto him.

So Joseph had two children during the seven years of plenty.

Verses 51-54:

And Joseph called the name of the firstborn Manasseh: For God, *said he,* hath made me forget all my toil, and all my father's house.

And the name of the second called he Ephraim: For God hath caused me to be fruitful in the land of my affliction.*

And the seven years of plenteousness, that was in the land of Egypt, were ended.

And the seven years of dearth began to come, according as Joseph had said: and the dearth was in all lands; but in all the land of Egypt there was bread.

Not only in Egypt, but in all the lands the famine came. What do you think happened in the other countries? They were in disastrous straits, starving.

Verses 55 and 56:

And when all the land of Egypt was famished, the people cried to Pharaoh for

---

*Joseph was indeed one of the great men of God of all times, and for it his descendants received a double inheritance in the Promised Land. Joseph's two sons, Manasseh and Ephraim, each headed a tribe. This was indeed a great honor, a double-portion blessing because of their father. See Genesis 48.

> bread: and Pharaoh said unto all the Egyptians, Go unto Joseph; what he saith to you, do.
>
> And the famine was over all the face of the earth: and Joseph opened all the storehouses, and sold unto the Egyptians; and the famine waxed sore in the land of Egypt.

What a tremendous key to Egypt's eventual deliverance. Joseph did not give away the food to the other countries. He did not even *give* it to the Egyptians. He *sold* it to them. A nation is to take care of its own people first and foremost, but this is not to be done through a welfare program or any system in which people are not expected to work to eat and live. Joseph, walking by revelation, *sold* the food to the Egyptians. Yet, as we shall see, his walk of wisdom is what enabled them to survive the terrible famine.

The God that provided for Egypt is the same God living today. God is always interested in saving people, whether it be as nations or individuals. God wants people to have life and to have it more abundantly; but in order for people to have abundance, they must operate the principles from God's Word. Only adherence to God's Word will sustain a nation and cause it to prosper.

Verse 57:
And all countries came into Egypt to Joseph
for to buy *corn;* because that the famine was
so sore in all lands.

Joseph never ran a giveaway program. Other
starving countries were expected to *buy* the food,
just as the Egyptians did. Was Joseph being
cruel? No, he was operating godly principles. A
giveaway program actually helps no one.

From these events recorded in God's Word
emerges the most glorious era in Egypt's history.
The wealth of all the world poured into Egypt
because of one man of God who knew by the
spirit of God how to direct that nation.

This brings us to a challenging and awesome
conclusion. Joseph lived in the Old Testament as
God's servant. He could not be born again of
God's Spirit as we are. Yet he, by revelation
from God, delivered a nation from what could
have been total annihilation.

Egypt was saved because the spirit of God was
upon one man. Today we have a great many
more people all over the world with the spirit of
God in them. What could happen in our country
and in our world if believing people just took a
stand for the integrity and accuracy of God's

Word and declared it in all its greatness, and then obediently carried it out?

We have the God-given opportunity and responsibility to shine as lights in our nation. Let us do as Joseph did in the Old Testament: Listen to God and faithfully carry out His words. Whenever "a man in whom the Spirit of God *is*" speaks God's Word and allows His power to flow, God and all His blessings become manifested. Not only is one's own country delivered from adversity, but it provides the example of obedience and hope for the entire world.

Chapter Nine

CHOOSE YOU THIS DAY

Joshua's entire life was a witness for God. We studied some of Joshua's life in chapter 7, "The Transfer of Leadership," observing him from the time he acted as a spy to search out the Promised Land to the time he took charge following Moses' death. Joshua had been a minister and a servant to the great Prophet Moses. And when Moses' death drew near, God instructed him to take Joshua to the tabernacle so that Joshua could be given the charge to lead the children of Israel.

Deuteronomy 31:7,8,14:
And Moses called unto Joshua, and said unto him in the sight of all Israel, Be strong and of a good courage: for thou must go with this people unto the land which the Lord hath sworn unto their fathers to give them; and thou shalt cause them to inherit it.

And the Lord, he *it is* that doth go before thee; he will be with thee, he will not fail thee, neither forsake thee: fear not, neither be dismayed....

And the Lord said unto Moses, Behold, thy days approach that thou must die: call Joshua, and present yourselves in the tabernacle of the congregation, that I may give him a charge. And Moses and Joshua went, and presented themselves in the tabernacle of the congregation.

When Moses and Joshua presented themselves before God, God told Moses to ordain Joshua and to make clear to the people that Joshua would be their leader when Moses died.

Moses did die on Mount Nebo after he had viewed Canaan, the Promised Land. Thus the reins of leadership passed to Joshua. Joshua assumed the leadership of the children of Israel and, after thirty days of mourning Moses' death, he immediately obeyed God's command to "arise, go" across the Jordan and begin claiming the land which God had vowed to give to Abraham's seed.

Joshua 3:7:
And the Lord said unto Joshua, This day will I begin to magnify thee in the sight of all

Israel, that they may know that, as I was with Moses, *so* I will be with thee.

God assured Joshua that He would establish him as the leader of the children of Israel. In order to magnify Joshua in the sight of Israel, God walled up the flooding waters of the Jordan River so that all Israel could pass over to the west side of that river into the Promised Land. Joshua, according to God's instructions, then set up memorial stones at the place where the priests who had carried the ark of the covenant had stood when the waters of the Jordan were "cut off."

This great miracle of crossing the Jordan on the dry riverbed was followed by Joshua's first victory in taking possession of the Promised Land at the city of Jericho. Joshua's success at Jericho was a result of his following God's directions to him, and following them exactly: The children of Israel compassed Jericho once a day for six consecutive days. On the seventh day, God had them walk around the city seven times. Then the priests blew their trumpets, the people shouted, and the wall of Jericho "fell down flat," just as God had promised.

After these two great miracles—the crossing of

173

the Jordan River and the conquering of Jericho
—Joshua continued to act on God's command to
rid the land of its inhabitants and have the
children of Israel take possession of it. But the
very next confrontation, the battle of Ai, was not
a success story. The army of Israel was defeated
by the army of Ai because, unknown to Joshua,
one Israelite warrior had disobeyed God at the
battle of Jericho. With this defeat at Ai, Joshua,
surprised and sorrowful, besought the Lord, ask-
ing why He had not helped them. God answered
in Joshua 7:12: ''...Neither will I be with you
any more, except ye destroy the accursed from
among you.'' Joshua was to destroy the man who
had taken spoil at Jericho. Not only the man, but
his entire household was to be destroyed because
of his disobedience to God's command. Again,
Joshua obeyed God, the army of Israel attacked
Ai, and this time was able to conquer it.

Over and over again Joshua proved himself
obedient to God's instructions to him, dividing
the land of promise among the tribes, appointing
cities of refuge, and establishing the Levitical
cities. He quelled a potential quarrel between the
two-and-a-half tribes on the east side of the Jordan and the rest of the tribes, and peace reigned
for the children of Israel.

Joshua lived a life pleasing to God. And as it became apparent to him that his life was drawing to an end, Joshua took one last step to assure that the children of Israel would remain faithful to God. I call this "Joshua's witness." The specific record of Joshua's witness occurs very near the end of Joshua's life when Joshua called all the tribes of Israel together at Shechem.

> Joshua 24:1:
> And Joshua gathered all the tribes of Israel to Shechem, and called for the elders of Israel, and for their heads, and for their judges, and for their officers; and they presented themselves before God.

Before he died, Joshua not only called together the children of Israel, but he called them to Shechem. Why Shechem? Not because the tabernacle was there, because it wasn't. The tabernacle was in Shiloh. Why did Joshua call the people to Shechem? For several reasons. Shechem was the first place in the Promised Land where God had told Abraham that the land was his. So Shechem was associated with God's promise to Abraham and His covenant with Abraham.* Shechem was

---

*Compare Genesis 12:6,7; and 17:1 with Joshua 24:2,3, 13,14.

also the place where Jacob had buried strange gods, according to Genesis 35:1-4. And Shechem lay between Mount Ebal and Mount Gerizim, the two mountains from which the blessings and the curses of the law were pronounced, according to Deuteronomy 27.

For all these reasons, Shechem was the most impressive place for Joshua to congregate the people of Israel to bring them into remembrance of the covenant and the law and to rebuild their commitment.

The people "presented themselves before God" at Shechem. This means that they presented themselves before God's spokesman and prophet, Joshua. Joshua then had the challenge of presenting God's Word to the people of Israel. God had done many great things for those people as they were led out of Egypt into the Promised Land, and Joshua reminded them of this.

> Joshua 24:11:
> And ye went over Jordan, and came unto Jericho: and the men of Jericho fought against you, the Amorites, and the Perizzites, and the Canaanites, and the Hittites, and the Girgashites, the Hivites, and the

Jebusites; and I [God] delivered them into your hand.

God said, "I delivered them [your enemies] into your hand." It wasn't the children of Israel who won the victories; it was God Who won them. And He used unusual and amazing ways to deliver them. Israel's deliverance from the Amorites is one example.

Verse 12:
And I sent the hornet before you, which drave them out from before you, *even* the two kings of the Amorites; *but* not with thy sword, nor with thy bow.

God has a great sense of humor and great resourcefulness. His method of defeating the Amorites was to have hornets sting their mighty armies.

Verse 13:
And I have given you a land for which ye did not labour, and cities which ye built not, and ye dwell in them; of the vineyards and oliveyards which ye planted not do ye eat.

I often think of how God has done things like this for us today—He has given us things which

177

we did not deserve, victories which we did not achieve, things that from our point of view we should never have had. God just handed them over to us.

After reviewing with the children of Israel what God had done for them, Joshua next reminded them of their responsibility to God.

> Verse 14:
> Now therefore fear [reverence, respect, hold in awe] the Lord, and serve him in sincerity and in truth: and put away the gods which your fathers served on the other side of the flood, and in Egypt; and serve ye the Lord.

The first command Joshua gave the people was to rid themselves of any other gods. Whenever anyone has a god other than the one true God, that person is in trouble. So long as Israel was faithful and served the one true God, God delivered them.

I know that God's Word is talking about literal idols here, and today you may not have an idol or a statue of a god. But you still can have a god other than the one true God. Your god could be a job, a social position, food, or a hobby— just anything that is more important to you than

178

doing God's will. What is first in your life? What is your god? Joshua told the children of Israel to get rid of anything that stood in the way of serving the one true God. If money is still more important to you than God, you have a god —money. That is what is meant by the expression, "Put your wallet on the altar. Dedicate it to God." You have to get to the place that there is only one God in your life, and that God is the true God, Jehovah, and He is the only one you will serve. He is the one to whom you are dedicated. Everything else in life is secondary. Matthew 6 tells us this.

Matthew 6:33:
But seek ye first the kingdom of God, and his righteousness; and all these things shall be added unto you.

The only way to real success is to have the one true God and to put Him first in your life. The decision to serve the one true God and no other gods was Joshua's concern in his final instructions to the children of Israel before he died.

Joshua 24:15:
And if it seem evil [wrong] unto you to serve the Lord [*Jehovah*], choose you this day whom ye will serve; whether the gods which

179

your fathers served that *were* on the other side of the flood [and those gods weren't powerful enough to keep us from leaving Egypt], or the gods of the Amorites, in whose land ye dwell [and those gods weren't powerful enough to keep us from subduing their followers and taking their land]: but as for me and my house, we will serve the Lord.

Joshua told the people to choose, to make a decision, whom they would serve. Jehovah had delivered them from the Egyptians and their gods, and Jehovah had delivered them from the Amorites and their gods, to cite just two examples of God's power having been abundantly manifested to them. The children of Israel could serve the other people's gods if they chose. But they also had the option of choosing to serve Jehovah, the one God Who had delivered them over and over again.

"...Choose you this day whom ye will serve...." We, too, have to make a choice. Are we really going to stand for God and His Word or are we just going to talk about it? We must make up our minds. Joshua had made up his mind when he said with great determination, "As for me and my house, we will serve the Lord."

With these words, Joshua set an example and a challenge for others to accept. Joshua and his house were determined to serve the Lord. The question still remained: Whom were the rest of the people of Israel going to serve?

> Verses 16-18:
> And the people answered and said, God forbid that we should forsake the Lord, to serve other gods;
>
> For the Lord our God, he *it is* that brought us up and our fathers out of the land of Egypt, from the house of bondage, and which [Who] did those great signs in our sight, and preserved us in all the way wherein we went, and among all the people through whom we passed:
>
> And the Lord drave out from before us all the people, even the Amorites which dwelt in the land: *therefore* will we also serve the Lord; for he *is* our God.

Once the people voiced their decision to continue serving Jehovah, Joshua could then give them further instructions for their walk before God.

> Verses 19 and 20:
> And Joshua said unto the people, Ye cannot

serve the Lord: for he *is* an holy God; he *is* a jealous God; he will not forgive your transgressions nor your sins.

If ye forsake the Lord, and serve strange gods, then he will turn and do you hurt, and consume you, after that he hath done you good.

This warning by Joshua is the Old Testament way of saying that when people turn away from God, they are no longer protected by Him. The Devil can then do as he pleases with them. The Devil may get an inroad into some of our lives at times, but the Devil's power over those born again is limited because God is always present within them.

Verses 21 and 22:
And the people said unto Joshua, Nay [we will not forsake the Lord]; but we will serve the Lord.

And Joshua said unto the people, Ye *are* witnesses against yourselves that ye have chosen you the Lord, to serve him. And they said, *We are* witnesses.

The people said to Joshua, who spoke for God, that they would be faithful to Jehovah. So

Joshua responded, "You yourselves are witnesses of the promise which you just made."

Verses 23-26:
Now therefore put away, *said he,* the strange gods which *are* among you [Some were still around.], and incline your heart unto the Lord God of Israel.

And the people said unto Joshua, The Lord our God will we serve, and his voice will we obey.

So Joshua made a covenant [an agreement] with the people that day, and set them a statute and an ordinance [a commandment] in Shechem.

And Joshua wrote these words in the book of the law of God, and took a great stone, and set it up there under an oak, that *was* by the sanctuary of the Lord.

Joshua made an agreement with the people and wrote it on a scroll. To put the covenant into writing after making an oral vow made a greater impact on the people's minds, and it became a source of reference and a reminder of their vow. The covenant, or agreement, was the commitment that Joshua, God's spokesman, had heard the people make: They would serve God and obey His voice. When the people were given a choice of whom they would serve, they answered Joshua in one voice, "We are going to remain faithful to Jehovah. We choose to serve Jehovah. And we are not going to allow our people to marry men and women who serve other gods. We guarantee that we are going to stand for the true God."

Joshua then wrote the commitment which Israel had made, and he "took a great stone"— the longest lasting and largest thing he could have used—and built a place where all the people could see the stone. This permanent marker was to be a constant reminder of their commitment to Jehovah, as witnessed by Joshua.

Joshua took the symbol of their commitment, a great stone, and placed it beneath an oak tree. The oak tree in the Bible symbolizes the presence of God. In Biblical times people would sit under an oak tree to pray. When a person in the Eastern culture wanted to ponder something or wanted to consider carefully a situation and make a decision, he would sit under an oak tree. Thus it was beneath an oak tree that Joshua chose to mark the children of Israel's very great and important decision to commit themselves to serve the Lord.

As years went by, the stone remained. The Word declares that these people were to teach the commandments to their children and to their children's children.* They would see the stone and be reminded that their forefathers had made a commitment to serve no other god but Jehovah only. This great stone was something they could see for years and years, and it would remind them of the covenant made there at Shechem.

Verses 27 and 28:
And Joshua said unto all the people, Behold, this stone shall be a witness unto us; for it hath heard all the words of the Lord which he spake unto us: it shall be therefore a witness unto you, lest ye deny your God.

So Joshua let the people depart, every man unto his inheritance.

Joshua sent every man back to his inherited

---

*Deuteronomy 6:6-9: "And these words, which I command thee this day, shall be in thine heart: And thou shalt teach them diligently unto thy children, and shalt talk of them when thou sittest in thine house, and when thou walkest by the way, and when thou liest down, and when thou risest up. And thou shalt bind them for a sign upon thine hand, and they shall be as frontlets between thine eyes. And thou shalt write them upon the posts of thy house, and on thy gates."

land which God had given him. He allowed the people to go back and reap the fruit of that which God had made available to them.

As believers we have only one life to live and to give, and we have to give our utmost for God's Highest. Our commitment to serve God releases God's blessing on our lives, just as it did in the time of Joshua. We have the freedom of choice to decide this day whom we are going to serve. I exhort you to make the same commitment with me: "As for me and my house, we will serve the Lord." This is the great decision around which all of our lives pivot. Commit yourself to serve God and Him only, and teach your children and your children's children to do the same. Hold to that commitment and enjoy the inheritance provided for you by God through Christ Jesus, and declare boldly, "As for me and my house, we will serve the Lord!"

Chapter Ten

THE WAY OF LIFE OR DEATH

Jeremiah, an Old Testament prophet, has been called the weeping prophet because he was always weeping over Israel when they turned away from God.* Regardless of what people may call those who seek God and His way, God still reveals Himself to the meek. And sometimes what God reveals is intended to give the unbeliever, who is meek, an opportunity to leave his spiritual darkness and the valley of death and to follow the way of life. Jeremiah was God's messenger to offer God's plan to the people of his day. "There are two ways before you," Jeremiah told the children of Israel. "One way is the way of life; the other is the way of death. Now you choose which you will follow. You choose your destiny."

I think we of The Way Ministry are again setting before the people of our time those two choices—the way of life and the way of death.

---

*Jeremiah 13:15-17; 22:9,10; 48:29-32.

Those who reject God's Word and those who deliberately abuse it are choosing the way of death. But those who come to God's Word, believe it, and act on it are choosing the way of life.

When spokesmen of God declare these two ways and make clear to people the two alternatives, people are not always pleased. They don't always want to hear the truth and may not appreciate those who speak it. Jeremiah and other prophets, some of whom are listed in Hebrews 11, were wonderful spokesmen of God who heard God's voice and who set before the people of their times the truth of God's Word. Hebrews 11 describes how some of these prophets and believers were treated in response to their speaking for God.

> Hebrews 11:37 and 38:
> They were stoned, they were sawn asunder [cut up into pieces], were tempted, were slain with the sword: they wandered about in sheepskins and goatskins [The skins of freshly skinned animals were sewed on them. When the skins dried, the bodies would be compressed inside.]; being destitute, afflicted, tormented;

(Of whom the world was not worthy:) they wandered in deserts, and *in* mountains, and *in* dens and caves of the earth.

These were men and women of God who in their day and in their time endeavored to carry out God's Word; they held it forth to the best of their abilities. The people's response to these men and women of God was what we just read. And people haven't changed. Some individuals, yes, but whole nations, no. We must still come to the position of again setting before people what I believe is the way of life for those who believe God's Word and the way of death for those who do not, regardless of their response to the person presenting the choice.

You set the Word before people and people make up their minds whether they want to believe it or whether they don't want to believe it. Those who believe it get the results of their believing. Those who do not believe it get the consequences of their unbelief. For those who believe, it is the way of life. For those who do not believe, it is the way of death.

In the Book of Jeremiah, we are certainly impressed by the number of times Jeremiah was instructed by God to offer the inhabitants of Judah a way of escape from the doom which their

189

unbelief would bring upon them. By chapter 19 of Jeremiah, where this study begins, God had repeatedly told Jeremiah to declare to the people of Jerusalem and Judah that unless they destroyed their idols and returned to worshiping Jehovah, they would be taken captive to Babylon for seventy years. Literal captivity would be their consequence for not heeding God's voice via the Prophet Jeremiah. Now, the people didn't want to hear this! They didn't want to rid themselves of their idolatry; they didn't want to change. So God once again told Jeremiah to go to the people of Jerusalem and pronounce their doom to them.

> Jeremiah 19:14 and 15:
> Then came Jeremiah from Tophet, whither the Lord had sent him to prophesy; and he stood in the court of the Lord's house [the Temple]; and said to all the people,
>
> Thus saith the Lord of hosts, the God of Israel; Behold, I will bring upon this city and upon all her towns all the evil that I have pronounced against it, because they have hardened their necks, that they might not hear my words.

Jeremiah's declaration of God's revelation to him—"I [God] will bring upon this city and

upon all her towns all the evil that I have pronounced against it"—was not news received with
appreciation and meekness. In the days of the
Prophet Jonah, the entire city of Nineveh
responded to a similar warning and penitently
turned to God. But the people of Judah rejected
the preaching of Jeremiah and felt no remorse,
refusing to hearken to God's Word. In fact, the
Book of Jeremiah continues this account by telling the abuse which Jeremiah had to endure for
having been God's spokesman.

> Jeremiah 20:1:
> Now Pashur the son of Immer the priest,
> who *was* also chief governor in the house of
> the Lord, heard that Jeremiah prophesied
> these things.

We are about to find out how this man Pashur
dealt with God and God's man, Jeremiah. Clearly
Pashur was a man of prestige and authority.
Besides being the son of a priest, thus having
status in the religious circles of his time, he was
also the "chief governor in the house of the
Lord," the Temple. What an elevated position of
leadership to have! Such religious and social
prestige!

But Pashur, the son of a priest and the chief

ruler of the Temple, was neither meek nor open to God and His Word as delivered by the Prophet Jeremiah.

> Verse 2:
> Then Pashur smote [*nakah*] Jeremiah the prophet, and put him in the stocks that *were* in the high gate of Benjamin, which *was* by the house of the Lord.

When Pashur heard that Jeremiah had prophesied Judah's doom, "Pashur smote Jeremiah the prophet." Jeremiah hadn't hurt anybody. He wasn't out stealing from people. He wasn't going around destroying property. And yet Pashur, this man of prestige and authority, a man highly respected by the vast majority of the people, smote Jeremiah the prophet, God's spokesman.

Now what do you think of when you read, "Pashur smote Jeremiah"? What exactly did Pashur do? Maybe you never gave it much thought. It's just a word, "smote." The Hebrew word for "smote" is *nakah*. Deuteronomy explains what this word means, which is translated "beaten" in Deuteronomy 25.

> Deuteronomy 25:2 and 3:
> . . . if the wicked man *be* worthy to be beaten

[*nakah*], that the judge shall cause him to lie down, and to be beaten [*nakah*] before his face, according to his fault, by a certain number.

Forty stripes he may give him, *and* not exceed: lest, *if* he should exceed, and beat [*nakah*] him above these with many stripes, then thy brother should seem vile unto thee.

Pashur forced Jeremiah to endure thirty-nine lashes with a whip. That's how Pashur smote Jeremiah. Then he had Jeremiah put into stocks, with his hands, his feet, and his neck locked between two large pieces of wood, at the high gate of Benjamin.

The high gate of Benjamin was at the north side of the Temple area, leading to the city. This gate was "by the house," the Temple. By punishing Jeremiah in the area of the house of Jehovah, Pashur made the prophet a public exhibition at the very place where God said He would meet His people. Pashur was making a mockery of God's spokesman, and therefore a mockery of God, in the very area of God's own House!

First of all, Pashur had Jeremiah beaten with thirty-nine lashes. Then he put him in stocks at the high gate of Benjamin, making him an example and causing fear in the people so that they would not believe Jeremiah's pronouncement of doom. If anyone believed what Jeremiah said, they would receive the same treatment he had received. Nobody would dare to listen to him, to follow him, or to join him.

Pashur left Jeremiah in the stocks all day and all night to punish and disgrace him and to spread fear and thereby to maintain control over the whole city.

> Jeremiah 20:3:
> And it came to pass on the morrow [the next day], that Pashur brought forth Jeremiah out of the stocks. Then said Jeremiah unto him, The Lord hath not called thy name Pashur, but Magormissabib.

Pashur was causing people to fear. Jeremiah told Pashur, "The Lord did not speak of you as 'Pashur,' meaning 'most noble.' That's not your name so far as God is concerned. Your name is 'Magormissabib,' 'fear all around.'" It took a lot of courage for a man in Jeremiah's position—having just been beaten, put in stocks, and publicly disgraced—to speak out with the greatness of the truth of God's Word at the

194

moment of his release. Would you have had that much boldness?

> Verses 4 and 5:
> For thus saith the Lord, Behold, I will make thee a terror [*magor*] to thyself [I'll make you have fear yourself], and to all thy friends: and they shall fall by the sword of their enemies, and thine eyes shall behold *it:* and I will give all Judah into the hand of the king of Babylon, and he shall carry them captive into Babylon, and shall slay them with the sword.
>
> Moreover I will deliver all the strength of this city [all the manpower], and all the labours thereof, and all the precious things [valuables] thereof, and all the treasures of the kings of Judah will I give into the hand of their enemies, which shall spoil them, and take them, and carry them to Babylon.

It was not God's will that this should happen to Judah, but the people caused it to happen by their unbelief, by their rejection of God, and by their treatment of God's prophet, Jeremiah, who spoke for God. When they rejected the way of life and treated Jeremiah with contempt, it was as if God were being treated with contempt.

Man can do a lot of things; but there is one thing he can't do and get away with—and that is to mock God. It may look like he's getting away with it at times, but don't be fooled. It looked that way here when Pashur was wielding authority. But circumstances change. Pashur's life wasn't over yet.

Jeremiah had the boldness to look directly at Pashur and say, "Look, you can put me in stocks, you can beat me, that's okay. But I want to tell you something: You and all Judah are going to suffer because you have not obeyed my warning."

> Verse 6:
> And thou, Pashur, and all that dwell in thine house shall go into captivity: and thou shalt come to Babylon, and there thou shalt die, and shalt be buried there, thou, and all thy friends, to whom thou hast prophesied lies.

Pashur could make a public mockery of the prophet. But in the end, the truth of God would indeed prevail. The prophesied end of Pashur, the powerful chief officer of the Temple, was death in Babylon along with his friends. The Word of the Lord was spoken clearly by Jeremiah, and that's exactly what happened.

After seeing the boldness of Jeremiah in the first six verses of Jeremiah 20, the next three verses in the King James Version seem out of character for him.

Verses 7-9:
O Lord, thou hast deceived me, and I was deceived: thou art stronger than I, and hast prevailed: I am in derision daily, every one mocketh me.

For since I spake, I cried out, I cried violence and spoil; because the word of the Lord was made a reproach unto me, and a derision, daily.

Then I said, I will not make mention of him, nor speak any more in his name. But *his word* was in mine heart as a burning fire shut up in my bones, and I was weary with forbearing, and I could not *stay*.

These three verses are hard to understand after observing Jeremiah's forthrightness in the preceding verses. A much better and a clearer translation of verses 7, 8, and 9 is found in Dr. George M. Lamsa's Aramaic translation:

Oh Lord, thou hast comforted me, and I am comforted; thou art stronger than I, and hast prevailed; I have become a laughing-stock daily, every one mocks me.

For at the time when I spoke and cried out, I spoke against the extortioners and against the robbers; because the word of the Lord has become for me a reproach and derision daily.

Then I said, I will not make mention of him [the Lord], nor speak any more in his name. But his word became in my heart like a burning fire kindling in my bones; and I sought to be patient, but I could not endure it.*

This is tremendous. How wonderful these words of Jeremiah are. Jeremiah praises God for being his comfort. "Lord, you've comforted me. I am at peace."

Within himself Jeremiah was as every human being would have been in his situation. He wanted to be respected, loved, and blessed. He wasn't speaking God's Word just because he wanted to make trouble. He spoke God's Word because that was the only thing he knew to do.

---

*George M. Lamsa, trans., *The Holy Bible from Ancient Eastern Manuscripts* (Nashville, Tenn.: A.J. Holman, 1957).

But then as he spoke God's Word, he was punished for it by people's reproach, derision, and mocking. As a human being, Jeremiah became discouraged. Who wants to be a laughingstock and suffer reproach? Jeremiah became weary of this, and his emotions almost overcame him. He thought that if he didn't mention Jehovah or speak in His name anymore, people would leave him alone. But then, Jeremiah declared, "His word became in my heart like a burning fire kindling in my bones." Jeremiah couldn't bear not to speak God's Word.

Worn down by the smiting, the ridicule, and the mocking, Jeremiah had wanted to close his mouth and stay out of trouble. But then just as he was going to withdraw and be quiet, God's Word became like a burning fire in his heart. God's Word welled up within Jeremiah. He could not keep silent. As God's Word burned in his heart and in his bones—his whole inner being—Jeremiah couldn't keep still. He had to speak what he was called by God to speak no matter what the consequences; otherwise, he said he could not have endured it.

Throughout the centuries, men have come and gone, but the Word of God has lived and will continue to abide forever. Jeremiahs come and go, but the Word of God that they proclaim

199

comes to pass. It's the Word of God that comes to pass. And it's the Word of God that stands no matter what men say, think, or do. Don't be fooled by the world. Do you think the people of the world have power? Man has no power. Man is like the grass of the field—here today and gone tomorrow. It's the Word of God that remains. It is God's Word which sets before mankind the two choices of life and death. Jeremiah, as God's spokesman, presented these choices to the inhabitants of Jerusalem and all Judah in his day.

Jeremiah 21:8:
. . . I set before you the way of life, and the way of death.

The choice is that sharp. You've got to make up your mind whether you're going to believe God's Word or whether you're going to believe the Pashurs who speak contrary to God's Word.

Hebrews 4:12:
For the word of God *is* quick [living], and powerful [energetic], and [the Word of God is] sharper than [or above] any twoedged sword, piercing even to the dividing asunder of soul [natural life] and spirit [spiritual life], and of the joints and marrow, and [the Word of God] *is* a discerner [critic; the

Word of God is the critic] of the thoughts
and intents of the heart [the mind of man].

The Word of God is the critic. Yet many people think that they are the judges of God and His
Word. Man always gets things backward when
he goes his own way.

You must make up your mind whether or not
you're going to walk for God and live according
to His Word. Whether or not you live according
to that Word, now and always the Word of God
is still your critic. We, of our own free will,
choose either the way of life or the way of death.
Pashur couldn't outsmart God by ridiculing the
person who spoke God's Word. Neither can we
outsmart God by devising our own ways and
working contrary to His ways. Rather, we need
to kindle the fire of God's Word in our hearts
and let it ignite our lives with the power of God.
Thereby we choose the way of life.

PART IV

GOD'S ORDER
FOR
QUALITY BELIEVERS

PART IV

GOD'S ORDER FOR QUALITY BELIEVERS

Quality believers are those followers of the Lord Jesus Christ whose lives are ordered in God's Word. It is evident that before anyone's life can be ordered in God's Word, that person must first acquire an accurate knowledge of God's Word. So it was with Zacchaeus in "Climbing High to Seek Truth." Zacchaeus sought the Lord Jesus Christ, gained a knowledge of the truth, and then ordered his life according to God's Word.

In "The Mark of Quality" we study Galatians 5 and 6 to find the qualities that characterize Word-oriented believers.

"The Light of Life" details the significance of light in God's Word. Light orders our lives both in a physical sense and in a spiritual sense.

The last chapter, entitled "Quickened Together with Christ," is a study of the wonderful and inspiring truths found in Colossians 2. Believers in

205

the Age of Grace are completely complete in Christ Jesus because of his accomplishments. God in His unfathomable grace and mercy tells us who we are in Christ Jesus and what great riches are available to us as God's children. How can we not fervently desire to have our lives established by a God Who loves us so dearly?

> Psalms 119:133:
> Order my steps in thy word: and let not any iniquity have dominion over me.

Understanding God's order should motivate all of us to order our steps more perfectly in His Word. Sin will have no dominion over us, and we will manifest God's will as quality believers.

Chapter Eleven

CLIMBING HIGH TO SEEK TRUTH

As we pass through life, we must climb ever higher and higher in our hearts and minds with the greatness of God's Word. We must always keep progressing to see more and more of God's Word and His promises manifested in our daily lives.

Luke 19 contains the record of a man who literally climbed high to see the savior. This is the account of Jesus and Zacchaeus, a story that always stirs the hearts of those hungering for God's Word.

> Luke 19:1:
> And *Jesus* entered and passed through Jericho.

The city of Jericho is northeast of Jerusalem, situated on the Jordan River. Frequently when Jesus traveled from Galilee to Jerusalem, he passed through Jericho. Luke 19 relates what occurred in one particular instance.

Verse 2:
And, behold, *there was* a man named Zacchaeus, which was the chief among the publicans, and he was rich.

This Zacchaeus was the chief among the publicans. Publicans were tax collectors. Zacchaeus was not just a common tax collector; he was *chief* in that area of Judea. Tax collecting then, even more than today, was considered a disreputable occupation. The Roman system of tax collecting in Judea and throughout the Roman Empire during Jesus' lifetime was known to be an abusive system, compounded by the dishonesty and extortion of the publicans associated with it. Many passages in the Gospels bring this fact to light, Luke 3 being one example.

Luke 3:12 and 13:
Then came also publicans to be baptized [by John the Baptist], and said unto him [John], Master, what shall we do?

And he said unto them [the publicans], Exact no more than that which is appointed you [or, "Don't take more than you're ordered to collect."].

It was not an uncommon practice for publicans

to demand more taxes than they were required to collect. For example, if a tax collector were instructed to collect $100 from you, he might inform you that you owed $120. He would collect $120, turn in the $100 to the Roman government, and put $20 in his own pocket.

Another reason that tax collectors were held in such low esteem was that these publicans, being Judeans, were virtually aiding the uncircumcised Romans at the expense of their own people. Publicans were dealing with and helping the foreign conquerors by doing Roman "dirty work."

The Gospel of Matthew gives an account of Jesus Christ's being confronted by a group of people on this same sensitive issue of taxation.

Matthew 22:17 and 18:
. . . [the people asked Jesus] Is it lawful to give tribute [head tax] unto Caesar, or not?
But Jesus perceived their wickedness, and said, Why tempt ye me, *ye* hypocrites?

In the situation recorded here, those questioning Jesus weren't sincerely interested in the truth; they were interested in trapping Jesus by catching him in his own statements. Nevertheless, we who are sincerely interested in learning can learn from Jesus' response.

Some of these wicked hypocrites tempting Jesus were Herodians, Judeans who supported Roman rule. Among them were probably publicans who were exacting more taxes than the law called for. Jesus knew who they were and caught them off guard with his wise response.

> Verses 19-21:
> Shew me the tribute money. And they brought unto him a penny.
> And he saith unto them, Whose *is* this image and superscription?
> They say unto him, Caesar's. Then saith he unto them, Render therefore unto Caesar the things which are Caesar's; and unto God the things that are God's.

For any nation there has to be some type of taxation. It is our responsibility as citizens and Christians to give to Caesar the things that are Caesar's and to God the things that are God's, and we must recognize the difference.

Just because tax collecting may be considered a vulgar occupation associated with extortion in an abusive system, that doesn't make everybody who collects taxes an extortioner. This is as true today as it was in the days of Jesus Christ.

I've explained this sidelight information about publicans in the first century in order for us to appreciate the great significance found in the account of Zacchaeus and Jesus in Luke 19. We need to understand the social implications of tax collecting and tax collectors.

Verse 2 of Luke 19 tells us that Zacchaeus was "chief among the publicans, and he was rich." Now people have read these two statements as if they were directly related. Some conclude that the reason Zacchaeus was rich was that he was a publican who collected more than was required, that he was extorting money from people. But does God's Word say that? No, it doesn't. It simply states that Zacchaeus was chief among the publicans and that he was rich. It doesn't say he cheated to get rich. This may have been a practice by other publicans, but it doesn't say that Zacchaeus did it. We have no right to read into this statement in Luke that Zacchaeus obtained his wealth dishonestly.

Publicans were tax collectors, just as some people today are farmers or plumbers or politicians or teachers. Just because a person is a rich plumber doesn't indicate that he is a corrupt

211

plumber who has obtained his wealth dishonestly. That's an unjustified assumption. Neither occupation nor wealth indicates dishonesty. All I know is that the Word of God says Zacchaeus was a publican and he was rich. We learn one other thing about Zacchaeus in this account and that is that he was motivated by a wonderful desire: He wanted to see Jesus.

> Luke 19:3:
> And he sought to see Jesus who he was; and could not for the press, because he was little of stature.

Zacchaeus wanted to see Jesus—who he was. Perhaps it was simple curiosity prompting him. The text doesn't say. But whatever the reason, at least he wanted to see Jesus. I wish that today, across our nation, there were more people who wanted to see Jesus. When people ask to see Jesus today, we've got to show him. When they want to see Jesus, who he is, we can show them God's Word and the greatness of Jesus Christ's position in the Word.

Zacchaeus wanted to see Jesus, but he couldn't. The reason he couldn't see him or get to him was for "the press." That doesn't mean the news media, such as newspaper, radio, or television reporters. "Press" means "numbers of people." There were so many people surrounding Jesus that Zacchaeus couldn't get a glimpse of him.

Verse 3:
...because he was little of stature.

Zacchaeus was short. The biggest thing about him was his desire to see Jesus.

Verse 4:
And he [Zacchaeus] ran before [ahead of where Jesus was walking], and climbed up into a sycamore tree to see him: for he [Jesus] was to pass that *way*.

Zacchaeus climbed up into a sycamore tree in order to get a view of this noted person, Jesus, whom people were talking about. Zacchaeus took the necessary action to fulfill his desire. That's very important. If you want to see Jesus Christ through God's Word, you need to move, take action. Zacchaeus took the initiative and climbed up into that sycamore tree.

The record that the tree Zacchaeus climbed was a sycamore tree is interesting information. A tree called "a sycamore" in the Bible is not the same as the common sycamore tree found here in America. The sycamore tree spoken of in the East in Bible times was a certain type of fig tree. A sycamore fig is specifically what the tree was. It is significant that Zacchaeus would climb this type of tree. Sycamore fig trees were despised; they bore a fruit that was fed to cows and pigs.* But Zacchaeus climbed one in search of spiritual nourishment from the Lord Jesus Christ, who is the greatest food of all time; indeed, he is the bread of life. Zacchaeus' climbing the despised sycamore fig tree was an act of great humility.

> Verse 5:
> And when Jesus came to the place, he looked up....

Zacchaeus was crouched in the sycamore fig tree looking down, while Jesus Christ looked up. Jesus Christ cared enough about this one man to stop amid all the hubbub and demands of the pressing crowd and speak directly to that one person.

I want to tell you, whenever there are men and women desiring to know the Lord Jesus Christ,

---

*K.C. Pillai, *Light through an Eastern Window* (New York: Robert Speller & Sons, 1963), p. 105.

they will have that desire met according to God's Word. Those people who hunger and thirst after righteousness *shall* (absolutely) be filled. That's right. What an example of fulfilling this promise from this record in God's Word.

Verse 5:
And when Jesus came to the place, he looked up, and saw him, and said unto him, Zacchaeus, make haste, and come down; for to day I must abide at thy house.

Did Jesus say, "Zacchaeus, you're a lowly, no-good publican"? Did he call, "Hey, Shorty"? No. How did Jesus know his name? The record doesn't tell us, but he addressed Zacchaeus directly. Zacchaeus had never before seen Jesus Christ, let alone ever had a conversation with him. How electrifying!

Since Zacchaeus could not see Jesus because of the crowd and his size, he climbed up into a sycamore fig tree to see him. Jesus came along, surrounded by masses of people, stopped, and said, "Hi, Zacchaeus. It's wonderful that you are looking for me. Come down now. I'm going to your house with you." What do you think Zacchaeus' heart did? I'll bet it picked up a few beats. I'll bet tears welled up in this surprised and blessed man's eyes. Zacchaeus couldn't conceive of Jesus' offer to him. "Me? Me? Me?" Jesus said, "Yes, you, Zacchaeus. Come on, make haste, come down. Today I'm going to spend time at your house." And do you know, Zacchaeus responded quickly and joyfully to Jesus' offer. It says so in verse 6.

Verse 6:
And he made haste, and came down, and received him [in his home] joyfully.

Zacchaeus made haste and received Jesus joyfully into his home. No one who is living dishonestly and cheating people, whose heart is of stone, would receive Jesus Christ joyfully. But Zacchaeus' heart and personal life must have been pure and at peace, for he readily received Jesus into his home.

Put yourself in the same place. Let's say you lived like the Devil, raised hell, ran around, and carried on. Then an outstanding and powerful believer came and said, "Come on, I want to spend the day with you." How would you feel? Terrible. Your inclination would probably be to make excuses and then decline the offer; the situation would make you too uncomfortable.

216

That is why I do not believe all the unsubstantiated things some people have suggested about Zacchaeus; such accusations cannot stand up against the truth of God's Word. I believe Zacchaeus must have been a wonderful man.

Verse 7:
And when they [the people around Jesus, perhaps including apostles, disciples, and others] saw *it* [that Jesus went to Zacchaeus' house], they all murmured, saying, That he was gone to be guest with a man that is a sinner.

The people murmured. They didn't speak in normal tones; they whispered, "How can Jesus, this great prophet, go to the house of and be the guest of a man who's a sinner?" How do you like that? The crowd didn't come right out and say to him, "Jesus, do you realize that you're eating with a bad guy?" No, they murmured behind his back.

While the people were carrying on in their ignorance, Zacchaeus was telling Jesus about himself.

Verse 8:
And Zacchaeus stood, and said unto the

217

> Lord; Behold, Lord, the half of my goods I
> give to the poor....

When Zacchaeus revealed this information, it gave a whole new perspective on this man. How many people do you know who give fifty percent of their incomes to help others? Zacchaeus gave that much. And he wasn't lying to Jesus, or Jesus would have known and reproved him. He said, "Lord, I give half of my goods to the poor."

> ...and if I have taken any thing from any man by false accusation [or extortion—if I've taken *anything* as a tax collector, anything from anybody illegally], I restore *him* [How much?] fourfold.

I want to tell you, Zacchaeus was a wonderful man! He was saying to the lord, "If I've taken anything from any man which I shouldn't have taken, Lord, I'd give back to him four times the amount that I took." Quite a tax collector. Yes, he was rich. But that was not all that characterized this man. He was also extremely charitable. He shared fifty percent of his goods with the poor. And he declared, "If I've extorted anything from anybody, I'll pay it back four times over." What a man!

That is why Jesus stopped at his house. He didn't stop there because Zacchaeus was an underhanded thief, a dishonest tax collector. As a publican, Zacchaeus would be despised by the public as a whole. He would be considered by many to have a disreputable occupation working for the Gentiles. Yet Jesus stopped with him that day because Jesus didn't live by stereotypes. He walked by his revelation from God, and he knew that Zacchaeus was not a wicked, underhanded, hard-hearted person. Jesus knew by revelation that Zacchaeus was a wonderful, honest man desiring to hear God's Word. And Zacchaeus' own words bore out that revelation.

Imagine Jesus Christ's coming to this man's house! A man whom he had never met before. It must have been exciting for Zacchaeus. A once-in-a-lifetime experience.

Verse 9:
And Jesus said unto him, This day is salvation come to this house. . . .

Why was salvation come to that house? Because the savior himself was there. Wherever the savior is, there is salvation. But why Zacchaeus' house?

...forsomuch as he also is a son of Abraham.

Do you know what a son of Abraham is? A believer. A person who, when God's Word is opened to him, hears the Word and believes it.* Zacchaeus was not only a blood descendant of Abraham, he was a believer. Jesus went home with him, shared his life with him, and taught him God's Word. Salvation came that day to Zacchaeus' house because a son of Abraham, a believer, came to know Jesus the Christ. What a wonderful record in God's Word.

Then comes Jesus' statement in verse 10, which reproved the murmurings spoken of in verse 7.

Verse 10:
For the Son of man is come to seek and to save that which was lost.

Zacchaeus had never before had the privilege of meeting Jesus. He had never before heard what you and I today would call "the message of salvation." Yet he wanted to see Jesus. So he climbed up in a tree. When Jesus saw him, he

---

*Galatians 3:7: "Know ye therefore that they which are of faith [believing], the same are the children of Abraham."

said, "Zacchaeus, come on down, and I'll spend some time at your house." There Jesus taught him God's truth, and Zacchaeus believed it. Jesus then said that the Son of man, Jesus Christ, was come to save those who were lost.

Jesus Christ is a physician of the soul. A physician is not needed when one is healthy. Jesus Christ comes to seek and to save, to give wholeness to those in spiritual need. He seeks those who are lost—men and women who need the Lord Jesus Christ. He has no problem extending himself to you and to me, because we are the people he came to seek and to save. Hebrews 7:25 says that Jesus Christ is "able also to save them to the uttermost that come unto God by him." Jesus Christ is always ready to meet you. He met Zacchaeus, who had climbed up in a tree to see him. Wherever there are men and women who really want to hear, Jesus Christ is always there.

There is no one so low that the arms of the Almighty are not underneath him. There is no one so high that the arms of the Almighty are not over him. And there is no one other than His Son who can save people. For there is no other name given among men whereby we must be saved.*

---

*Acts 4:12: "Neither is there salvation in any other: for there is none other name under heaven given among men, whereby we must be saved."

Ladies and gentlemen, whatever you have to do to know the Lord Jesus Christ, do it. Wherever you have to go to learn about him, do it. The one great driving force of your soul should be to know Jesus Christ. Who is he? The only way you'll ever know who Jesus Christ is is to come to God's Word. The Word makes known Jesus Christ. The Word tells you who he is. It is that Word which brings you to a knowledge of salvation.

What do you need to hear? God's Word.* Jesus Christ was that Word, the Living Word, who met Zacchaeus that day in Jericho. And he brought Zacchaeus to the great reality of being a believer, because Jesus was willing to teach him and Zacchaeus was meek to learn. If you want to experience the truth of God's Word, climb high to seek truth. God always has and always will seek out and teach those who are looking to Jesus Christ as their savior and lord.

---

*Romans 10:17: "So then faith *cometh* by hearing, and hearing by the word of God."

Chapter Twelve

THE MARK OF QUALITY

As children of God and imitators of Jesus Christ, each of us wants to live a quality Christian life. The type of quality we want is the God-defined quality which He unfolds for us in His Word. Quality Christian lives are "fruit-bearing" lives. They are fruit-of-the-spirit-filled lives. Galatians 5 enumerates the fruit of the spirit.

> Galatians 5:22:
> But the fruit of the Spirit...

The topic is "fruit of the Spirit." Spiritual fruit comes as a result of operating the manifestations of holy spirit. To understand this, let's examine the production of natural fruit. Let's take apples, for example. To grow an apple, first an apple seed must be sown. When the life processes in that seed begin to function, a seedling sprouts and grows. As the tree reaches maturity, it bears fruit—apples. Similarly, if each one of us is going to have the fruit of the spirit, we've first got to have the spirit, which is seed. Then this spirit must be cultivated by our "walking by the spirit," by our operating the manifestations of the spirit. The end result of the utilization of the manifestations of the spirit is spiritual fruit.

Now what is this fruit that results? There are nine qualities listed as the fruit of the spirit in Galatians 5.

> Galatians 5:22-26:
> But the fruit of the Spirit is love, joy, peace, longsuffering, gentleness, goodness, faith,
> Meekness, temperance: against such there is no law.
> And they that are Christ's have crucified the flesh with the affections and lusts.
> If we live [*zaō*] in the Spirit, let us also walk [*stoicheō,* proceed] in [by] the Spirit.
> Let us not be desirous of vain glory, provoking one another, envying one another.

Our mark of quality is our having the fruit of the spirit manifested in our lives. The mark of quality is a fruit-of-the-spirit-filled life which is the result of walking with the manifestations of the spirit.

Now, I couldn't have that mark of quality if I didn't have Christ in me. "Christ in me" means that I have been born again—a spiritual birth. And that new birth is seed. It is the new creation by God's Spirit. Yet that seed is simply potential. It is the cultivation of that seed which will result in quality lives. Just what kind of life are you manifesting? What are you doing in your walk? Do you have that mark of quality that God's Word says you should have as a born-again son or daughter of God? Galatians 6 begins to show what this walk looks like, how one recognizes the fruit of the spirit.

> Galatians 6:1:
> Brethren, if a man be overtaken in a fault, ye which are spiritual, restore such an one in the spirit of meekness; considering thyself, lest thou also be tempted.

Let those who are spiritual do what? Restore. We're not to tear down believers who have a fault. The word "restore" basically means "to correct." All Scripture is profitable for doctrine, reproof, and correction.* In this verse, we are

---

*II Timothy 3:16: "All scripture *is* given by inspiration of God, and *is* profitable for doctrine, for reproof, for correction, for instruction in righteousness."

225

told to restore the person who has a fault by correcting him or her in the spirit of meekness.

We must also understand what is meant in verse 1 by "ye which are spiritual." From the context in Galatians 5:16-26, we note that a person is to walk by the spirit and thus bear the fruit of the spirit. So, "ye which are spiritual" must have the mark of quality, have a fruit-of-the-spirit-filled life. Further light can be found in I Corinthians 14 concerning those who are "spiritual."

> I Corinthians 14:37:
> If any man think himself to be a prophet, or spiritual, let him acknowledge that the things that I write unto you are the commandments of the Lord.

It is in this section of I Corinthians 14 that God commands Christians to speak in tongues. He also tells them that in believers' meetings they should interpret their message in tongues and prophesy and operate all the manifestations of the spirit decently and in order according to His Word. If we are spiritual, we shall recognize that these are commandments of the Lord; and if we are not spiritual, we'll argue about them and conclude that they are not commandments of the

Lord. So when Galatians 6 speaks of a spiritual man, that spiritual person (according to I Corinthians 14 and Galatians 5:16-26) is one who recognizes and lives by the instructions written in the Church Epistles, which include manifesting the holy spirit and bearing the fruit of the spirit.

Galatians 6:1 gives specific instruction regarding the person who is spiritual. It says that if you are a spiritual person, you don't push down and stomp on a person overtaken in a fault. If you are a spiritual person, you correct the person in the spirit of meekness. Meekness is a fruit of the spirit, demonstrated by freedom from haughty self-sufficiency. Why "restore"? "Lest thou also be tempted"—to not walk according to God's Word—and get caught in a fault, or offense. This is a walk of correcting in meekness. It is an attitude of gentle correction like, "God's Word says this. And because I love you, I want you to have the best and I know you want to have the best, so I'm correcting you." You correct and restore such a one who is "overtaken in a fault."

> Galatians 6:2:
> Bear ye one another's burdens [*baros*], and so fulfil the law of Christ.

Here is a verse people have difficulty with

because it says, "Bear ye one another's burdens," and then verse 5 says, "For every man shall bear his own burden." This sounds like a contradiction. The difficulty here is in the English translation.

In verse 2 the word "burdens" is the Greek word *baros,* meaning "a burden or pressure that can be shared or lightened by another." We are to help one another. That's love. If you restore someone in meekness, you share God's Word with them. You help to carry their burden. And as you do that you fulfill the law of Christ.

What is the law of Christ? Many times people talk about the law of Christ, but they don't know the practical side of it. Christ gave this law shortly before his crucifixion.

> John 13:34:
> A new commandment I give unto you, That ye love one another; as I have loved you, that ye also love one another.

You no longer love only in response to someone's loving you. You are to love others as Jesus Christ loves you. These are two totally different concepts. Believers are to love one another with the love of God, as Christ loved us.*

Galatians is addressed to the believer, not to the unsaved, the unbeliever. You can't restore an unbeliever. He needs salvation, not restoration. He needs to be born again. But we who are born again are to bear each other's loads. We are to help one another wherever we can. That is what the word "burden" in Galatians 6:2 means. It says, "Bear ye one another's burdens." It doesn't say, "Think about it." It says, "Do it." It doesn't ask you whether you like the way I look or the way I comb my hair. It says that if I am your brother you should help me carry my load. If you are my brother or sister, then it is my responsibility likewise to help you carry yours.

Galatians 6:3:
For if a man think himself to be something, when he is nothing, he deceiveth himself.

---

*The Epistle of I John also tells us this. I John 4:20 and 21: "If a man say, I love God, and hateth his brother, he is a liar: for he that loveth not his brother whom he hath seen, how can he love God whom he hath not seen? And this commandment have we from him, That he who loveth God love his brother also."

In the context now we are still talking about bearing burdens. Verse 3 refers to those who feel that they are self-made people. They feel they need no help in bearing their own burdens, and, conversely, they do not help others with theirs. That is definitely contrary to God's Word. This type of man never fulfills the law of Christ. A person is never really self-made. The Word says he deceives himself because he does indeed need believers to help him carry his burdens, *baros*.

> Verse 4:
> But let every man prove his own work, and then shall he have rejoicing in himself alone, and not in another.

A man is to examine his own work to see if it is his own responsibility and if he has met his responsibility. If he has, then verse 4 says he shall have rejoicing in himself alone, and not in a "burden" shared with another, as in verse 2.

> Verse 5:
> For every man shall bear his own burden [*phortion*].

The word "burden" here is *phortion*, not *baros*. In verse 2, "burdens," *baros*, is a weight that can be shared. This "burden" in verse 5 is something that cannot be shared by another person. Nobody else can assume it or help you with it. That is the difference in these two verses. Two entirely different Greek words are used for these two entirely different situations. For instance, there are some things in my life which other people can help me with. But then there are other weights in my life that I alone must carry. When another person can help carry my burdens, the word is *baros*. But in those areas where no one can help me carry my burdens, or my responsibilities, the word *phortion* is applicable.

The accuracy of God's Word is astounding! There is no contradiction between verse 2 and verse 5 of Galatians 6. Isn't the accuracy of this Word wonderful.

> Verse 6:
> Let him that is taught in the word communicate unto him that teacheth in all good things.

"Let him that is taught in the word...." The word "in" should be omitted. "Let him who is taught the Word...." "Word" is *logos* in the Greek, the same word used in John 1. "Communicate unto" is "share with," referring to material

231

and financial support. "Let him who is taught God's Word share with him who teaches in all good things."

Verse 7:
Be not deceived....

In other words, don't get fooled. When a person is deceived, the deception has to come from the adversary because he is the great deceiver.* So if you are deceived, you've been listening to the wrong source, because you can't be deceived by the God and Father of our Lord Jesus Christ. God does not deceive; He enlightens.

Verse 7:
Be not deceived; God is not mocked: for whatsoever a man soweth, that shall he also reap.

A great and deep truth is found here in that word "mocked." It is a graphic orientalism concerning insults. If, in Biblical culture, you really wanted to insult someone, you would tap him or her on the cheek. It wasn't a slap, but rather just

---

*Revelation 12:9: "And the great dragon was cast out, that old serpent, called the Devil, and Satan, which deceiveth the whole world...."

a touch on the cheek with the left hand, the hand of cursing. This was a great insult. Another great insult was to spit at a person. Yet another type of insult was to literally turn up your nose. The word "mocked" here in Galatians 6:7 is "to turn up one's nose in scorn." Be not deceived; God is not someone at whom you can turn up your nose. In other words, a person can't make a fool of God. The orientalism emphasizes that, without fail, a man reaps what he sows.

Don't try to turn up your nose at God in scorn because what you really are in your heart will be manifested, "for whatsoever a man soweth, that shall he also reap." If you don't carry anybody else's burden, nobody is going to help you carry yours. If I am your brother and you are not willing to help me when you are capable of it, you are turning up your nose at God. How can we say we love God when we don't treat each other as brothers? We do just the opposite. That is what "sowing" refers to in this context of talking about the walk. The mark-of-quality Christian who really loves God and exemplifies it in his day-by-day walk sows good seed, such as restoring a person overtaken in a fault and sharing the burdens of others.

Verse 8:
For he that soweth to his [own] flesh shall of

233

the flesh reap corruption; but he that soweth to the Spirit shall of the Spirit reap life everlasting.

To "sow" is to plant. When I love you with the love of Christ, I am sowing. When you walk with the love of Christ, you are sowing. And what you sow you get back, you reap. If you give out hell, that is what you are going to get back. If you give out bitterness, that is what you are going to get back. If you give out criticism, that is what you are going to get back. If you give out the love of Christ, that's what you are going to get back. You reap whatever it is that you are giving out. In the context, sowing to the spirit is to walk by holy spirit. It is a walk.

Verse 8:
...he that soweth to the Spirit shall of the Spirit reap life everlasting.

To "reap life everlasting" is beyond simply having eternal life. Eternal life is acquired by grace, not by works.* It is a gift. But here in Galatians 6 "life everlasting" is talking about

---

*Ephesians 2:8 and 9: "For by grace are ye saved through faith; and that not of yourselves: *it is* the gift of God: Not of works, lest any man should boast."

Romans 6:23: "For the wages of sin *is* death; but the gift of God *is* eternal life through Jesus Christ our Lord."

reaping the results of our walk, our works. What is the reaping? The reaping is the reward. When you take your corn to market, you get paid for it. When you do a day's work or a week's work in a factory, you get paid. The reaping is that pay. So as believers who walk by the spirit, we also get our pay. But when? "Life everlasting" shows that the pay comes both now and continuing on from now. In its usage in verse 8, "life everlasting" includes all the rewards of walking on the Word both now and throughout eternity. Christianity is so dynamic because not only do we have the joy of the abundant life now, but we have all eternity to enjoy the rewards of having sown to the spirit.

I tell you, people who do not want to accept the Lord Jesus Christ and live God's way have no idea of what they are missing. This is the only life of joy and blessing and peace. My friend Rufus Mosely used to say, "This walking with God is so fantastic that it's heaven going to heaven, even if there is no heaven when you get there." So make up your mind whether you'll walk God's way, the way of His Word, or whether you'll walk the way of the world. Every man and woman decides what kind of seeds he or she plants.

Verse 9:
And let us not be weary in well doing. . . .

We must walk the Word and walk the Word and walk the Word. We can't be weary in doing that. We have the joy of living by God's Word now, and we will have the joy of reaping the rewards of our quality walk throughout all eternity.

> Verse 9:
> And let us not be weary in well doing: for in due season [proper time] we shall reap, if we faint not.

God says that you are going to reap if you don't faint, if you don't become weary in well doing. To faint is to give up and say, "Oh, I am so tired of being good to people." At that point we lose the greatness of bearing each other's burdens. The conviction of God's Word must be in our souls to serve even when our emotions nag at us not to serve.

> Verse 10:
> As we have therefore opportunity, let us do good unto all *men,* especially unto them who are of the household of faith.

We are to do good to everyone, as the occasion arises, "as we have opportunity." The rest of the verse says we are to do good "especially unto them who are of the household of faith." We are

236

to spend our time, energy, and resources doing good to the believers. However, we do not do evil to anyone, but rather do good to everyone as we have the occasion. This is the epitome of a quality life for a believer. This is a fruit-of-the-spirit-filled life.

Paul ends the epistle to the Galatians by pointing out the physical marks he has received of men.*

> Galatians 6:17:
> From henceforth let no man trouble me: for I bear in my body the marks of the Lord Jesus.

The word "marks" in the text is the Greek word *stigma,* the brand or mark of a slave. When a slave in the East was purchased, he had his owner's brand, *stigma,* put on his earlobe or forehead. Paul uses the "marks" figuratively to show that his master, the Lord Jesus, was made known by the marks of quality evident in Paul's life. The *stigma* didn't mean that Paul had been branded with a literal branding iron. A person could be physically branded all over his body, yet that doesn't show or mean that he loves God. You could write across your forehead, "I love

---

*II Corinthians 11:23-27.

God," but that doesn't mean you really do love God. What have you got on the inside?

Paul lived by the spirit and therefore manifested the fruit of the spirit. He lived a life of dedication with love and service. For his bold witness Paul was thrown in prison and finally executed, but he never renounced the truth of God or His Word. That is a mark of quality.

What have you got on the inside? How is that new creation, the Christ in you, being manifested in the senses world? Are you bearing spiritual fruit? Do you bear the burdens of others? Do you restore with meekness those who stumble? Do you walk by the spirit? Are you faithful in well doing? Do you do good to all men, but especially to the believers? All of these things give you the wonderful mark-of-quality life, a life lived for God Almighty.

We must walk according to God's Word; we must stay committed to God and His Word. Let us stand for God's Word—stand with meekness, with love, with faithfulness. Then our lives will clearly show the mark of quality. When we bear in our lives that mark of quality, then we are showing that God's brand, the most excellent brand of all, is on us.

238

Chapter Thirteen

THE LIGHT OF LIFE

Throughout the Word of God we see the importance of light, both physical light and spiritual light. In the first chapter of Genesis when God was preparing this earth for us, the first thing He said was, "Let there be light."

Genesis 1:3:
And God said, Let there be light: and there was light.

And one of the last things God reveals in the Book of Revelation also regards light. The setting is the new heaven and the new earth.

Revelation 22:5:
And there shall be no night there; and they need no candle, neither light of the sun; for the Lord God giveth them light: and they shall reign for ever and ever.

The greatness of all that God ever did and ever will do between the time of Genesis 1:3 and

Revelation 22:5 is to make light available to man, because God is Light.

> I John 1:5:
> This then is the message which we have heard of him, and declare unto you, that God is light, and in him is no darkness at all.

Throughout His Word it is recorded that God is Light. Now how can anybody say that he has light if he doesn't know the true God, the source of light? Nobody can say that he has light until he knows God. God is Light and if anybody is ever going to have light, he must have a relationship with God, he must plug into the source.

Since God is Spirit* and therefore cannot be seen, the only way we by our senses can learn about God is to go to His written Word, which is in the senses realm. If God is Light, so is His Word. The light of God's Word makes known God Who is Light. Without the light of God's Word, people will never know God, and they will continue to walk in darkness. They may say, "We have light," but this cannot be true. The fact that somebody says he has light is sometimes far removed from his actually having it.

---

*John 4:24: "God *is* a Spirit: and they that worship him must worship *him* in spirit and in truth."

I John 1:7:
But if we walk in the light, as he is in the
light,* we have fellowship one with
another....

If I live or "walk" in the light, God and I have
fellowship. If you walk in the light, God and you
have fellowship. And as we have fellowship with
God, our Light, we have a luminous life.

When believers see the greatness of God's light
and really live it, their lives are blessed, their
families are blessed, their communities are blessed.
So when believers are scattered all over the globe
blessing it, the world will see light, because God
is Light and His light is in the believers.

II Timothy 1:7:
For God hath not given us the spirit of fear
[cowardice]; but of power, and of love, and
of a sound mind.

God did not give us the spirit of cowardice,
"but of power, and of love, and of a sound

---

*Manuscript 1850 (thirteenth century) omits the words
"walk" and "as he is in the light." The remaining words
allow the verb "walk" by ellipsis: "But if we [walk] in the
light, we have fellowship." MS 1851 (tenth century) reads,
"But if we walk, as He is, in the light we have fellowship."

mind.'' God makes people powerful, loving, and able-minded. God makes winners, not failures. God is in the business of delivering people, not defeating them. He gives people sound minds, minds with judgment. And we, as God's people who have been given sound minds, must renounce our former unsound ways.

> II Corinthians 4:1 and 2:
> Therefore seeing we have this ministry, as we have received mercy, we faint not;
> But [we] have renounced the hidden things of dishonesty [the shameful, secret things]. . . .

Do you know what the hidden, shameful things are? No, they do not include smoking behind the barn. The hidden, shameful things are deliberate plans by people to promote their dishonesty in order to deliberately fool others about God's Word. How do they get in this sorry state?

> . . .not walking in craftiness, nor handling the word of God deceitfully. . . .

They walk in unscrupulous conduct and falsify the Word of God—these are the hidden things of dishonesty.

242

Having this ministry, we don't faint; we don't become weary of our responsibility. But because we have received mercy, we have renounced the hidden, shameful things—living unscrupulously and falsifying or handling the Word of God deceitfully. Because of what God has done for us, we clean up our lives and we handle the Word of God truthfully.

> ...but by manifestation of the truth commending ourselves to every man's conscience in the sight of God.

Instead of walking in craftiness and handling the Word of God deceitfully, we commend ourselves to every man's conscience, or belief of what is right. Conscience is nothing but habit patterns of thought which people establish in their lives. Your conscience bothers you because of a habit pattern you've established. When you put on the mind of Christ and train your conscience after the doctrine of God's Word, then your conscience will guide you with that Word. God's Word will be the habit pattern for keeping your everyday life on track.

Verse 3:
But if our gospel be hid, it is hid to them that are lost [perishing].

This "gospel" is the gospel of the deliverance of God. The word "hid" is "veiled." At a wedding you can tell there is someone under the bridal veil, but not until the bride gets to the altar and the veil is removed from her face can you really see her face. This is the veiling of the gospel to them that are perishing. The gospel is veiled to the lost. They can't see it well enough to believe it. Verse 4 then tells who is responsible for the veiling and who the lost are.

Verse 4:
In whom the god of this world hath blinded the minds of them which believe not....

Satan has blinded those who are perishing by keeping them from the true Light. He is in the business of blinding people's understanding so that they cannot clearly see the Word of God. Sometimes he demonstrates his own counterfeit light so brightly that it blinds people, or sometimes he makes everything contrary to God's Word look enticingly beautiful. But the whole purpose behind Satan's deeds is to blind people and keep them from the true Light.

Verses 4 and 5:
...lest the light of the glorious gospel of

244

Christ, who is the image of God, should shine unto them.

For we preach not ourselves, but Christ Jesus the Lord; and ourselves your servants for Jesus' sake.

Satan blinds the eyes of some who don't believe, so that the gospel of Christ won't light up their lives.

Verse 6:
For God, who commanded the light to shine out of darkness, hath shined in our hearts, to *give* the light of the knowledge of the glory of God in the face of Jesus Christ ["through the face," a figure of speech meaning "through the work that Jesus Christ did"].

We are the living reality of the presence of the power of God, endeavoring to rightly divide the Word, setting men and women free. We walk so that the light of the glory of God in us can be seen by others.

Now this does not mean that we are no longer capable of making mistakes. As a matter of fact, God's Word teaches that we are going to make mistakes. But when we do make a mistake, it is not a deliberate, crafty perpetration of wrongly dividing the Word. Our mistakes are simply a matter of not knowing or doing better. Maybe next week we'll know more of God's Word, and then we'll change. That is what life is all about.

> Verse 7:
> But [For] we have this treasure [this light of the knowledge of the glory of God] in earthen vessels, that the excellency of the power may be of God, and not of us.

This great treasure which we have is "the light of the knowledge of the glory of God," spoken of in verse 6. This most valued treasure of God is found in earthen vessels. These "earthen vessels" are our bodies. We have this precious treasure in our physical bodies. God contrasts so dramatically the earthen vessel with the excellency of His power. What a contrast! How dynamic the juxtaposition.

With this knowledge of the glory of God, we can come to the point in life that we totally trust God to take care of us and to lead us. We hold forth the greatness of the Word to our friends, our loved ones, and everyone else with whom we come in contact. Every place we go, we talk the Word. Do you have anything better to talk about? No. So talk about the best, God's Word. If there is anything the world really needs today, it is the Word of God. They don't need giveaway programs, they don't need rehabilitation programs, they don't need armaments. They need the Word. All these other things may have some use, but without God's Word man's real, basic need cannot be met. Only God's Word will truly satisfy. We must stand up and proclaim His Word. The light of the glory of God is the treasure that we have and that we want to share. We have only one life to live and give, and we may as well give our utmost for His Highest.

Let's look at a few usages of "light" in the Word, beginning in Matthew 5 in order to gain a greater understanding and appreciation of God as light and us as His light in the world.

Matthew 5:14-16:
Ye are the light of the world. A city that is set on an hill cannot be hid.

Neither do men light a candle [lamp], and put it under a bushel, but on a candlestick [a pillar]; and it giveth light unto all that are in the house.

Let your light [not your negatives, not your doubts, not your fears, not your worries] so shine before men, that they may see your good works, and glorify your Father which is in heaven.

247

We are the lights of the world. Suppose we don't always live according to the Word's way. Suppose we don't act as children of light. Do we get down on ourselves and stay there? No, we get back into fellowship with God* and get back to living His Word and radiating His light.

> John 8:12:
> Then spake Jesus again unto them, saying, I am the light of the world: he that followeth me shall not walk in darkness, but shall have the light of life.

Jesus Christ is the light; he was God's Word in the flesh. The person who follows God in Christ Jesus doesn't walk in darkness, but "shall [absolutely] have the light of life." Jesus Christ is the light; and you are the light when you live God's Word and witness to it. People must get to the light of God through His Word in order to have life. Otherwise they are in darkness, dead in trespasses and sins.

> Ephesians 5:8:
> For ye were sometimes [once] darkness [blind],

---

*I John 1:9: "If we confess our sins, he is faithful and just to forgive us *our* sins, and to cleanse us from all unrighteousness."

248

but now *are ye* light in the Lord: walk as children of light.

God is the one Who delivered us from blindness. He's the one Who took the darkness out of our souls. God is the one Who made us what the Word says we are. Because of what Jesus Christ did, we walk as children of light for we are sons of God.

I Thessalonians 5, in speaking of the return of Christ, contains this great truth.

I Thessalonians 5:5:
Ye are all the children of light, and the children of the day: we are not of the night, nor of darkness.

That's right. You are not of darkness, you are not of the night—you are children of the light, you are children of the day. And if people want to see the light, they've got to look at you. So give them some light to look at, because you have the knowledge of the Word to share with people, and that Word is light for them.

Philippians 2:13 and 14:
For it is God which worketh in you both to will and to do of *his* good pleasure.

> Do all things without murmurings [complaining] and disputings [arguing about it].

The text literally reads, "For it is God Who is at work in you." God is at work within you. To murmur, or complain, is to say, "Look, I have been out witnessing for three days and nothing has happened." Is God dead? Remember Noah? He witnessed for a while—in fact, he witnessed for 120 years!—and he didn't give up. If he had given up on the revelation God gave him, he would have missed the boat ride. Sometimes people have difficulty standing even momentarily for the true God. You won't have that problem if you know the Word and believe the Word. What is the result when you don't complain or argue about doing God's will?

> Verses 15 and 16:
> That [In order that] ye may be blameless and harmless, the sons of God, without rebuke [without blemish], in the midst of a crooked and perverse nation [generation], among whom ye shine as lights in the world;
> Holding forth the word of life....

You shine as lights in the world. Don't put your light of truth under a bushel. Walk on that light. Talk about it. Hold forth the Word of Life.

The Light of Life is God's Word. It gives light, making it possible for men and women to be born again of God's Spirit, to be filled with the holy spirit, to walk on the greatness of God's Word, and to shine as lights. We hold forth that Word of Life.

God has called us to be His lights and to radiate His Word across the world. So walk with your head high and your shoulders back, with joy in your soul, because you have the light of God within you. Wherever you are, with God in Christ in you, there is that same radiance, that same glowing light, in you. Rise up and stand tall, not because of who you are, but because of what God has made you. You have the light of life which cannot be extinguished and which needs to shine forth in these crooked and perverse times to draw people to the Light.

Chapter Fourteen

QUICKENED TOGETHER WITH CHRIST

As I see God's Word growing in the hearts and lives of our people, I am immeasurably thankful to God for His goodness and His grace. I often think of how the Apostle Paul must have rejoiced as he traveled and taught God's Word in the first century. I, too, rejoice and am deeply grateful for all who are making a stand for the accuracy and integrity of God's wonderful, matchless Word. God's Word gives the same vibrancy of life right now as it did when Jesus Christ himself walked on this earth.

Recall with me the wonderful record in the Gospel of Luke which tells of an occurrence the day after the resurrection of our lord and savior Jesus Christ. Jesus, on the road to Emmaus, joined two men who were discussing recent occurrences in Jerusalem. After walking with these men for a little distance, Jesus Christ related important information to them. Luke 24:27 tells us, "And beginning at Moses and all the prophets,

253

he expounded unto them in all the scriptures the things concerning himself.''

My, how I wish I could have been one of those two men. Wouldn't that have been thrilling to have Jesus Christ in your company explaining to you the scriptures which relate to himself, beginning with Moses and continuing throughout the Old Testament!

After Jesus Christ left them, these two men expressed their great excitement by exclaiming, ''Did not our heart burn within us, while he talked with us by the way, and while he opened to us the scriptures?'' Isn't that beautiful! You see, when the truth of God's Word is opened to us, our inner hearts become alive, like burning coals. God's Word is so thrilling, so exciting, so motivating.

The record in Luke 24 also states, ''And their [the two men's] eyes were opened.'' That is exactly what happens to us, too, when the Word of God becomes known, unfolded, to us. Our eyes need opening just as the two men's were opened on that road to Emmaus. And because God has such great care and concern for us who are seeking to know more about Him, He is constantly opening our eyes, illuminating our minds and hearts, and broadening our vision.

To see God's great care and concern for us we need to understand the truth found in the second chapter of Colossians. Let's begin with verse 1.

> Colossians 2:1:
> For I would [desire] that ye knew [were fully knowledgeable of] what great conflict [*agōn*] I have for you, and *for* them at Laodicea, and *for* as many as have not seen my face in the flesh.

The word "conflict" is the Greek word *agōn* which was associated in Greek literature with athletes who competed in the Olympic games. This word *agōn* means "care," "concern." The greatest care and concern were given to the training of these athletes so that they might compete at their maximum potential. Paul's desire was that the believers at Colosse and Laodicea be fully knowledgeable of the great care he had for them, even for those who had not seen his face in the flesh. This is the kind of care we must build in our lives for one another. We must have an earnest concern for God's people, even for those we have not seen.

You see, if Christ had not cared and loved us, we could not love. But now we are able to love.

255

God loved us when we were unlovable, dead in trespasses and sin; and many times we, too, must love even the unlovable. Sometimes we love *because of* and sometimes *in spite of,* but the important and necessary thing is that we *do* love one another. As born-again believers who are filled with the power of God and who believe God's Word, you and I must meet people's needs until they learn how to go to God to get their own needs met. We allow people to hitchhike on our ability to manifest God's power until they learn to manifest the power of God in their own lives. We have to have great love and concern.

This second chapter of Colossians is telling us that *things* are to be used and *people* are to be loved. We can use things to advance toward our goals, but we never use people.

Consider this: If God could so love me through Christ Jesus that He could save me to the uttermost—that I who was dead in trespasses and sins could be made alive, that He would cast my sins from me and remember them no more—is there any person in this world whom I cannot forgive? I have no problem forgiving other people when I consider the great grace with which God forgave me. And if you really know what God in Christ did for you, then you have no problem helping someone else so that Christ can do the same

256

redemptive, healing work for them. That's the tenderness, that's the concern we must have for all people everywhere.

Verse 2 tells why we need to have that care and concern for people.

> Verse 2:
> That their hearts might be comforted, being knit together in love, and unto all riches of the full assurance of understanding, to the acknowledgement of the mystery of God, and of the Father, and of Christ.

What a tremendous verse of scripture. An expanded translation of this verse would be: "We have this care for people so that their hearts might be comforted and encouraged, being united with one mind in one spirit for the glory of God by the manifested love of God which has been shed forth in our hearts by holy spirit, to the end that we altogether utilize, with full conviction, what we have learned by carefully listening to and thoughtfully reflecting upon the Word of God, with the ultimate goal of absolutely knowing the Mystery of God (Who is our Father) and of Christ (who is the head of the Church)."

This desire to comfort and encourage was also the reason Paul sent Timothy to Thessalonica.

I Thessalonians 3:2:
And sent Timotheus [Timothy], our brother, and minister of God, and our fellowlabourer in the gospel of Christ, to establish you, and to comfort [encourage] you concerning your faith.

Timothy was the most loyal, the most dedicated, the best-equipped person for Paul to send into a situation like Thessalonica. You wouldn't send your least qualified believer; you would send the best that you had into a demanding situation, and Thessalonica was difficult. So it was agreed that Timothy, "our brother and a minister of God," was the right person to send to Thessalonica. Timothy was also diligent, hardworking, and knowledgeable of the Word of God. These were necessary qualifications.

"...To establish you...." You see, getting born again is just the start. There are many people in the world who are born again of God's Spirit but who have had no teaching, no establishing, no building of the depth of God's Word in them. That's why this word "establish" is so meaningful. Those born again need to be established, which means "strengthened," "made firm," made solid in God's Word.

258

"...And to comfort you...." Establish and comfort. When people become solid on God's Word, it naturally follows that they will be comforted. The Greek word for "comfort" also means "encourage" and "exhort." Timothy was both to establish them and also to exhort or encourage them.

"Concerning" is "for the advantage and benefit." Timothy was to establish and encourage the Thessalonians for the advantage and benefit of their believing, *pistis*. Paul expressed this same encouragement to the Colossians.

> Colossians 2:3-5:
> In whom [In which, the Mystery] are hid all the treasures of wisdom and knowledge.
>
> And this I say, lest any man should beguile [deceive] you with enticing [persuasive] words.
>
> For though I be absent in the flesh, yet am I with you in the spirit, joying and beholding your order, and the stedfastness of your faith [believing] in Christ.

Paul says, "Watch out for those persons who seek to lure you away from God's Word, those who move you away from it by enticing words.

259

Yet be comforted and encouraged to know that I am speaking in tongues for you, and I am joyful over the steadfastness of your believing.'' Paul was always blessed when believers were faithful, like these believers in Colosse and those of Thessalonica.

> I Thessalonians 3:6:
> But now when Timotheus came from you unto us, and brought us good tidings of your faith and charity, and that ye have good remembrance of us always, desiring greatly to see us, as we also *to see* you.

When Timothy returned to Paul after visiting the believers in Thessalonica, he "brought us good tidings of your faith [believing] and charity [the love of God in the renewed mind in manifestation].'' That was the spiritual condition of the Thessalonians. These were the people about whom Paul had been greatly concerned, wondering if they, under persecution and ongoing affliction, were standing faithful. And when Timothy came back, he brought glad tidings of their believing and of their walking with the love of God in the renewed mind in manifestation. Their believing and love is the first point made in this verse.

The second point in I Thessalonians 3:6 pertains to their attitude. "...And that ye have good remembrance of us always...." The word "always" means "continuingly," not just at one moment, but continuing. They continued having good memories of Paul, Silas, and the rest of the believers, holding them in high esteem.

The third point in this verse concerns their mutual affection. "...Desiring greatly to see us, as we also *to see* you." "Desiring greatly" means "wanting with an intense desire." This shows the great affection of the Thessalonians for Paul. "...To see us, [even] as we also *to see* you." The Greek word for "as" means "even as" and indicates their mutual affection for each other, their mutual desire to get together with each other.

The combination "you" and "us" is used four times in this verse: Timothy "came from you unto us," number one; "brought us good tidings of your faith and charity," number two; "ye have good remembrance of us always," number three; "desiring greatly to see us, as we also *to see* you," number four. Four times these words occur together in the same verse. Such mutual appreciation, love, desire, and respect must be maintained between the leaders and believers if they want the greatness of God's Word to really live.

I Thessalonians 3:7:
Therefore, brethren, we were comforted over you in all our affliction and distress by your faith.

The word "comforted" here again means "encouraged." Brothers, we were encouraged "by your faith," by your believing or through your believing. "We were encouraged, in our outward distresses and our afflictions from other people, because you stood faithful."

This same mutual love and faithfulness is what Paul was writing about in the second chapter of Colossians.

Colossians 2:6:
As ye have therefore received Christ Jesus the Lord, *so* walk ye in him.

"As ye have therefore received Christ Jesus the Lord, *so* walk...." This doesn't say we are to relax after we've received Christ Jesus. Obviously, since we are saved and have eternal life, we are going to heaven. But is that all there is to life: get saved and tread water until the return of Christ? Not at all. Just as we've made Christ Jesus our lord, so we walk. And it is a minute-by-minute walk. How do we walk? Verse 7 tells us.

262

Verse 7:
Rooted and built up in him, and stablished
in the faith, as ye have been taught, abound-
ing therein with thanksgiving.

"Rooted...." That is number one in the
walk. The believer must be rooted. Jesus Christ
shows the importance of being rooted in
Matthew 13.

Matthew 13:20 and 21:
But he that received the seed into stony
places, the same is he that heareth the word,
and anon [immediately] with joy receiveth it;
Yet hath he not root in himself, but dureth
for a while: for when tribulation or persecution ariseth because of the word, by and by
[immediately] he is offended [he stumbles].

This man heard God's Word and had great joy
over it. But he had no root, and therefore endured only for a little while. When a problem
arose, he immediately fell away, because he had
no root.

So we see that in order to begin walking for
God, we have to be rooted. Otherwise when
someone questions or attacks the Word of God,
we won't stand very long. Some people may

question you, "What do you know about God's Word?" They'll challenge, "Who are you to talk to a graduate of a theological seminary? Surely ministers and theologians know more than you." The real question is this: Do they know God and His Word better than you do? They may be more knowledgeable of Plato, Aristotle, and Freud, but what about God's Word? Where are the treasures of knowledge and wisdom? In God's Word! So we need to get rooted in His Word. We must drive that Word into our minds. We need to read the Word itself, listen to tapes on the Word, read anything that is rightly divided on the Word, memorize the Word. We've got to be rooted. That's number one.

Number two, according to Colossians 2:7, we have to be built up. You cannot have a tall oak tree without having a highly developed root system. What's the point of the vast root system of an oak tree, if the trunk, limbs, branches, and twigs aren't equally developed? What's the point of being rooted in God's Word if nothing else is manifested in our lives? If you as a believer never go any further than just putting down roots, what can be accomplished? A believer must get rooted in the Word, but then he or she must grow and mature, "be built up," in the knowledge and wisdom of the Word. Being built up is step number two.

Not only are we to be rooted and built up in Christ, but according to Colossians 2:7, we also are to be established in the faith. An established tree is one that is at its peak of maturity. All the leaves are out, and the tree is in full bloom. Similarly, an established believer is one who has withstood the test of time and has come to maturity, full fruition. "Established" in the Greek is elsewhere in the King James Version translated "confirmed." One who is established is confirmed, steadfast, fixed, immovable, certain, and firm.

We are established, Biblically speaking, when we have grown up in Christ to the degree that we are manifesting the greatness of what God is. We are bearing fruit. We are not blown about with every wind of doctrine. We are not excited about the Lord one day and gloomy and depressed the next. We've got to get so established in God's Word that nobody can move us off center—as if we had cement poured around our feet, ankle-deep, and we stood still until the cement set. We just can't waver on God's Word. We must be cemented in His Word—rooted, built up, and established. That's what it takes to be minute-by-minute, year-after-year representatives for God. That's the walk. That's the talk.

I want you to observe two such representatives of God told about in Acts 16.

> Acts 16:4 and 5:
> And as they [Paul and Timothy] went through the cities, they delivered them the decrees for to keep, that were ordained of the apostles and elders which were at Jerusalem.
>
> And so were the churches established in the faith, and [as they were established they] increased in number daily.

As it says of Paul and Timothy, so should it be with you as a mature believer: The churches will be established and the numbers will increase daily.

And again in I Corinthians 3 observe two men who were established.

> I Corinthians 3:6:
> I [Paul] have planted, Apollos watered; but God gave the increase.

I Corinthians 3:6 says that in Corinth Paul had planted the seed of God's Word and Apollos had watered, but who gave the increase? God. Who is going to do the planting and watering today? Believers who walk and believers who speak God's Word. And as we walk, God gives the increase to the seeds we plant and water.

> Colossians 2:7:
> Rooted and built up in him, and stablished in the faith, as ye have been taught, abounding therein with thanksgiving.

There is only one way for people to begin to be rooted and built up and established and that is for somebody to teach them. So, in order to get people rooted, built up, and established, you need to teach as you have been taught.

"...Abounding therein with thanksgiving." Thanksgiving and "thanksliving" go hand in hand. Your thanksgiving to God causes thanksliving. Live the Word with thanksgiving and joy! You can't expect to be effective witnesses for God unless you live His Word. You can't just talk the Word; you have to live the principles of the Word or you won't last.

Now verse 8 of Colossians 2 begins with an "unfriendly dog" sign: "Beware." You have to watch out or beware (be aware) in order to maintain your walk in Christ Jesus.

267

Verse 8:
Beware lest any man spoil [*sulagōgeō*] you through philosophy and vain deceit, after the tradition of men, after the rudiments of the world, and not after Christ.

"Beware lest any man [any person] spoil...."
"Spoil" is *sulagōgeō,* which means "to carry off as plunder or booty." Don't let the adversary carry you away as the plunder of battle. It's not the rotten or spoiled apples the devourer looks for. It's the good apples that are seized by the enemy. The adversary expends his best efforts to keep you from being a bold witness for God. The adversary is not interested in the godless; he's interested in getting God-loving people and carrying them away as plunder.

"Beware lest any man spoil you through philosophy...." Philosophy is world wisdom. There are a lot of men and women who are tremendously keen with world wisdom; but we know from the Word of God that true wisdom and knowledge come from God. The great treasures of wisdom and knowledge lie with God, not in worldly wisdom. So beware, for you are going to be confronted with world wisdom.

The next thing to beware of is "vain deceit." "Vain" is "empty" in the Greek and "deceit" is

268

"misrepresentation"—in other words, intentional manipulation. "Philosophy" and "vain deceit" are tied together by the conjunction "and" because these two go hand-in-hand. They are both ego inflaters. They are "after the tradition of men."

To see the contrast between the greatness of God and the traditions of men, go to Matthew 15.

> Matthew 15:1 and 2:
> Then came to Jesus scribes and Pharisees, which were of Jerusalem, saying,
>
> Why do thy disciples transgress the tradition of the elders? for they wash not their hands when they eat bread.

The scribes and Pharisees, who made up part of the Temple hierarchy, were confronting Jesus Christ with the problem his disciples were causing by not washing their hands before eating. Washing the hands before eating was a "tradition of the elders."

> Verse 3:
> But he [Jesus Christ] answered and said unto them, Why do ye also transgress the commandment of God by your tradition?

269

So tradition can and often does transgress the commandment of God. And which of the two is the more important—the tradition of the elders or the commandments of the Lord? The answer is obvious. In verse 6 of Matthew 15 Jesus concludes, "Thus have ye made the commandment of God of none effect by your tradition." When tradition takes preeminence over God's Word, the commandments of God become ineffectual.

Then Jesus said to the people in the record of Matthew 15, "*Ye* hypocrites." Are you surprised that Jesus would say something so harsh? Didn't he love people? He certainly did; yet he called these people hypocrites. Remember the "beware" of Colossians 2:8? You must be aware of the tricks of tradition.

> Matthew 15:7 and 8:
> *Ye* hypocrites, well did Esaias prophesy of you, saying,
> This people draweth nigh unto me with their mouth, and honoureth me with *their* lips; but their heart is far from me.

"This people draweth nigh unto me with their mouth, and honoureth me with *their* lips...." They may say the right words, "but their heart is far from me." Were they religious? Were they sincere? They certainly were. But being religious or sincere is no guarantee of truth. God doesn't look on appearances; He looks on the heart —and "their heart is far from me."

Verse 9:
But in vain they do worship me, teaching *for* doctrines the commandments of men.

Did they, the people whom Jesus was addressing, worship? Oh, yes. They had candles, they had the altar properly arranged, they wore the right garb, they prayed at the right time, the organ introduction was melodious, and the psalms were read with the proper inflection. Everything looked so right, except for one thing—their hearts were far from God. Thus, they worshiped in vain. So what did they teach with their hearts far removed from God? They taught the commandments of men as their doctrine, not the Word of God.

Therefore Colossians 2:8 says, "Beware lest you be taken as plunder by worldly wisdom, by misrepresentation according to the tradition of men, according to the principles of the world, and not after Christ."

271

Colossians 2:9:
For in him [in Christ] dwelleth all the fulness
[full to capacity] of the Godhead bodily.

Notice the word "Godhead." This verse accurately says, "For in Christ dwelleth all the
fullness of that head God." And there is only
one head God. There are two gods, but there is
only one head God and that is the Father of our
Lord Jesus Christ. The other god is the god of
this world, and he is certainly not head God.

Jesus Christ was the first person mentioned in
God's Word who had without measure all that
God could make available at that time. Every
other person upon whom God had put His spirit
was given the spirit in a measured, specific
amount. Look at John 3.

John 3:34:
For he [Jesus Christ] whom God hath sent
speaketh the words of God: for God giveth
not the Spirit by measure *unto him*.

"...For God giveth not the Spirit by measure...." Jesus Christ then could operate to the
maximum all the manifestations of the spirit
available to him: prophecy, word of knowledge,
word of wisdom, discerning of spirits, faith

(believing), miracles, and gifts of healings. However, there were two manifestations he did not have—speaking in tongues and interpretation of tongues, because they were not available until Pentecost. That is why all the fullness of God, as full as it could be, dwelled in Christ. The "fullness of God" is everything that God can make available. Today we have the fullness of God in us and we can operate all nine manifestations. Jesus Christ could operate only seven. Everything that God could make available at that time, Jesus Christ had.

> Colossians 2:10:
> And ye are complete in him [Jesus Christ], which is the head of all principality and power.

"And ye are complete...." If you had one little thing missing, you wouldn't be complete. And you are complete because of what God did in Christ Jesus our lord and savior. And if Christ is the head and you have Christ in you, then that puts Satan right under your feet. You belong to God, and Satan has absolutely no rights over you or over your Christian brothers and sisters. You can extinguish all the fiery darts of the adversary because you have more power than he has.

Ephesians 1 corroborates this.

273

Ephesians 1:3:
Blessed *be* the God and Father of our Lord
Jesus Christ, who hath blessed us with all
[every] spiritual blessings in heavenly *places*
[in the heavenlies] in Christ.

God has blessed you with every spiritual blessing and has made you complete in Christ. God
was in Christ and Christ is in you. God in Christ
in you makes you complete in him. You are complete in him with every spiritual blessing.

Colossians 2:10 further says, "...which
[Jesus Christ] is the head of all principality and
power." We are completely complete in Christ
who is head over all principalities and powers.
Now consider this: If Christ is the head of all
principalities and powers, and if you are complete in Christ, are you powerful, are you more
than a conqueror? God in Christ in you gives you
the power to manifest the more abundant life
because you are over all principalities and
powers.*

---

*Ephesians 6:12: "For we wrestle not against flesh and
blood, but against principalities, against powers, against
the rulers of the darkness of this world, against spiritual
wickedness [wicked spirits] in high *places* [from on high]."

Born-again believers do not wrestle against flesh and
blood, against people; they wrestle only against spiritual

Colossians 2:11:
In whom [In Christ] also ye are [were] circumcised with the circumcision made without hands, in putting off the body of the sins of the flesh by the circumcision of Christ.

The covenant of circumcision was a covenant of blood. God said to Israel, "Okay, you are mine; I'll protect you. You've given your blood. We have a covenant, and I will not break the covenant of blood." So long as Israel walked on the commandments of God, there was literally nobody who could harm them. But Colossians 2:11 says that we were circumcised with the circumcision made without hands, which was putting off the body of the sins of the flesh.

Our circumcision is the getting rid of the body of the sins of the flesh. The body of the sins of the flesh was circumcised from us because Christ bore our sins. It was Christ's act, not our own, that put us into the blood covenant. We've just never seen this Word and the greatness of what we have in God in Christ, and the privilege we have of sharing it.

---

power. We are to deal with causes, not symptoms. And the causes of problems are principalities, powers, wicked spirits from on high. And since Christ is head of all principalities and powers and we have Christ in us, we are more powerful than Satan and can overcome him and the power he wields.

275

Verse 12:
Buried with him in baptism, wherein also ye
are risen with *him* through the faith of the
operation of God, who hath raised him
from the dead.

"Buried with him in baptism...." Do you
know what that baptism is? Christ's burial.
Frequently baptism does not refer to being im-
mersed in water. "Baptism" means "to purify or
cleanse." In this context it's going into the grave
with Christ. When he went there, we went with
him. "Buried with him in baptism, wherein also
ye are risen with *him*...."

We not only were circumcised in his crucifixion
and baptized in his death, but when God raised
Christ, we got up with him. You and I were raised
with Christ. "...Risen with *him* through [by
way of] the faith [believing] of the operation
[*energeia,* energy] of God, who hath raised him
from the dead." When Christ arose, we arose
with him. Jesus Christ believed that God would
raise him from the dead, and we believe the
same. That's the believing of Colossians 2:12.
Ephesians 1 adds even more knowledge to this.

Ephesians 1:18-23:
The eyes of your understanding being

enlightened; that ye may know what is the hope of his calling, and what the riches of the glory of his inheritance in the saints,

And what *is* the exceeding greatness of his power to usward who believe, according to the working of his mighty power,

Which he wrought in Christ, when he raised him from the dead, and set *him* at his own right hand in the heavenly *places* [the heavenlies],

Far above all principality, and power, and might, and dominion, and every name that is named, not only in this world, but also in that which is to come:

And hath put all *things* under his feet, and gave him *to be* the head over all *things* to the church,

Which is his body, the fulness of him that filleth all in all.

Thus Colossians 2 says that we were circumcised, buried, and raised with Jesus Christ; and Ephesians 1 says that we ascended with him and are seated with him. We are completely, completely complete! We are equipped; we've got it. Not because of who we are, but because of what God did in Christ when He raised him from the dead and set him at His own right hand.

When Jesus Christ got up, we got up with him; when he ascended, we ascended with him; when he sat down at the right hand of God, we sat down with him. It's already fulfilled.

> Colossians 2:13:
> And you, being dead in your sins and the uncircumcision of your flesh, hath he quickened together with him, having forgiven you all trespasses.

"And you, being dead in your sins...." You are no longer dead *in* your sins, but dead *to* them. You were dead *in* your sins before you were born again. But when you were born again of God's Spirit with Christ in you, you became dead *to* them. Each of us is born into this natural life dead in trespasses and sins, and the only way God can raise us up is by our confessing with our mouths the Lord Jesus Christ and believing that God raised him from the dead, as Romans 10:9 and 10 instructs us. Then we are given remission of sin and God puts His spirit in us, which is God in Christ in you, which is eternal life. We are no longer dead *in* trespasses and sins, but rather we become dead *to* trespasses and sins.

278

After God forgives us of all trespasses, Colossians 2 further explains what He does with all the accusations which were against us.

> Verse 14:
> Blotting out the handwriting of ordinances that was against us, which was contrary to us, and took it out of the way, nailing it to his cross.

I wondered about the meaning of this verse for fifteen or twenty years, realizing I did not understand it. I also had a problem with Isaiah 40. Verse 1 says, "Comfort ye, comfort ye my people, saith your God." The word "comfort" here means to soothe people, to give them peace and serenity. But the second verse of Isaiah 40 continues, "Speak ye comfortably to Jerusalem [God's people], and cry unto her, that her warfare [appointed time] is accomplished, that her iniquity [sin] is pardoned: for she hath received of the Lord's hand double for all her sins."

"...Comfort ye my people....Speak ye comfortably to Jerusalem...." Tell them that God is going to double their sin on them. Now how can you comfort someone if they are going to receive double for their sins? That doesn't make sense! Bishop K.C. Pillai finally explained to me what the "doubled" sin of Isaiah 40 is, and then I understood the phrase "blotting out the handwriting of ordinances" of Colossians 2:14.

In Old Testament times a part of the judiciary system was the elders at the gate. These were older men, experienced and wise in human affairs. They were selected from the foremost men of the community and were known for their honesty and good judgment. A person who became an elder at the gate was held in high esteem. He became responsible for making sound judgments and decisions regarding disputes of any kind. These elders at the gate were required to "sit" at certain appointed times, and if the city dwellers had disputes or problems, they were to present them at those times. Civil disputes and problems were settled in this manner.

Now, suppose an Israelite went bankrupt. He would have to report to the elders at the gate. The elders would make out a statement of bankruptcy which listed everyone to whom the debtor owed money. When the elders had finished writing down all the creditors, they would nail this bankruptcy notification on the gates of that city. It was posted as a constant public reminder of the debtor's dilemma and shame. Day after day this notice would hang on the gate of that city until all the debts were paid.

At any time during the posting of the debt a person could come along and act as a benefactor. He might walk in the gates and read the bankruptcy notice. Maybe he knew the debtor or his family. So the benefactor would go to see the elders at the gate and say, "I want to pay in full everything which is contrary and against this debtor," and then he would pay the debts. So what would the elders at the gate do with the bankruptcy notification? They would take it down and "double" it. That means they would fold it over so that the writing of indebtedness was inside and no one could see what had been against the debtor. Then the elders did something else. They wrote the former debtor's name on the outside of this doubled paper, and once more they would take the folded sheet and nail it to the gate of the city. Thus everybody would know that all the debts, all that which was contrary to the debtor or against him, had been fully paid.

In Isaiah 40 Israel had their sins doubled. "Comfort ye, comfort ye my people...for she hath received...double for all her sins." A benefactor, namely, the Lord God, paid for their sins and gave them a clean, doubled paper on the gates.

281

Similarly, Colossians 2:14 says, "Blotting out the handwriting of ordinances that was against us, which was contrary to us, and took it out of the way, nailing it to his [Jesus Christ's] cross." Jesus Christ who knew no sin became sin for us so we could become the righteousness of God in him. He paid our debts, and then God went a step better and blotted them out. He completely expunged, or erased, those things that were against us because Jesus Christ paid the price on the cross. Therefore, there is no record of the charges against us, only that all debts have been paid. Jesus Christ took the reproach which was against us. It was nailed to his cross. Isaiah 53:6 says, "All we like sheep have gone astray; we have turned every one to his own way; and [but] the Lord hath laid on him [Jesus Christ] the iniquity of us all."

> Colossians 2:15:
> *And* having spoiled [*apekduomai*] principalities and powers, he made a shew of them openly, triumphing over them in it.

This Greek word for "spoiled" means "having put off from himself," what he bore for us. He who knew no sin became sin for us. Then he put off from himself (spoiled) the sins, which were the principalities and powers. And he made a show of the principalities and powers openly, triumphing over them when God raised him from the dead.*

Now comes more important information for believers to bear in mind.

Verses 16 and 17:
Let no man therefore judge you in meat, or in drink, or in respect of an holyday, or of the new moon, or of the sabbath *days:*
Which are a shadow of things to come; but the body *is* of Christ.

Let no man judge you under the Old Testament law because you are not under that Old Testament law; you are in the Body of Christ during the Age of Grace. The Old Testament law was only a shadow of the greater law of the spirit of life in Christ Jesus, which is now in effect.

Verse 18:
Let no man beguile you of your reward in a voluntary humility and worshipping of angels, intruding into those things which he hath not seen, vainly puffed up by his fleshly mind.

---

*Ephesians 4:8: "Wherefore he saith, When he ascended up on high, he led captivity captive, and gave gifts unto men."

"Let no man beguile you...." The words "beguile you" mean "defraud you." Salvation is of grace and reward is of merit. Don't let anyone cheat you of your prize by involving you in his religious rituals, putting you under the tradition of men, and feeling proud of it, vainly puffed up.

> Verse 19:
> And not holding [fast] the Head [Who is the head? Jesus Christ.], from which all the body by joints and bands [bonding, putting together] having nourishment ministered, and knit together, increaseth with the increase of God.

The expression "knit together" in verse 2 of Colossians 2—"hearts might be comforted, being knit together in love"—is repeated here. We are to hold fast to the head, knowing that the whole body, having nourishment ministered by the bonded joints, increases. We minister God's Word to each other and thus the Body of Christ is nourished and grows. Every believer is part of that Body, and each of us goes forth to minister. Having received nourishment, we are knit together in the Body with every joint bonded together and contributing. One believer will be very strong in one area of practice, and another one

284

will be very strong in some other area; we complement and support each other. That is being knit together. It takes all the parts of the Body, each carrying out its unique function, to make the Body function properly. I Corinthians 12:21 expresses this image so clearly: "And the eye cannot say unto the hand, I have no need of thee: nor again the head to the feet, I have no need of you." Somebody has to be an eye, someone else a wrist, a thumb, or an index finger. What would happen if we were all the same part of the Body?

I may never particularly appreciate my fingers until one of them is sore. It's remarkable that when I hit my thumb with a hammer, my whole body feels the shock. Before hitting and irritating it, I'm not even conscious that I have a thumb. And it doesn't hurt for just that moment, but for some time following. The Body of Christ is like that. If one member is hurt, we all hurt. All the parts in the spiritual Body are interdependent just as in the physical body.

Members act in different and varied capacities in the Body. But each is only a part of that Body, and each must do his job to the best of his ability so that the whole Body can function effectively. If anybody does not function in his calling, the Body as a unit is hurt. Every member in particular is important. And when each member is

285

functioning, the Body increases with the increase from God. This is dynamic growth.

> Colossians 2:20:
> Wherefore [Because of this] if ye be dead [if ye died] with Christ from the rudiments [systems, principles] of the world, why, as though living in the world, are ye subject to ordinances.

If we died with Christ from the systems of the world, why do we allow ourselves to be subject to them again? Why, as though living in the world, are we dogmatized again to ordinances? What kind of ordinances are meant? God's Word goes on to explain this.

> Verses 21 and 22:
> (Touch not; taste not; handle not;
> Which all are to perish with the using;) after [according to] the commandments and doctrines of men?

These dogmatic ordinances are "after the commandments and doctrines of men." The "touch not; taste not; handle not" types of man-made ordinances corrupt the user. Why do we then subject ourselves to those rules which are after the commandments and doctrines of men? Remember Matthew 15? The Pharisees taught "*for* doctrines the commandments of men." When we worship according to men's commandments and doctrines, what kind of worship is it? Vain. It says in Matthew 15:9: "In vain they do worship me."

Colossians 2:23:
Which things have indeed a shew of wisdom in will worship, and humility, and neglecting of the body; not in any honour to the satisfying of the flesh.

Man's ordinances "have indeed a shew of wisdom." But that kind of wisdom is natural man's wisdom which, when studied earlier, we found of very little value because true knowledge and wisdom come from God. Man's ordinances and religious rituals do not "honour [have any value] tó [with a view to, toward] the satisfying [*plēsmonē,* filling up] of the flesh." Man's ordinances and religious rituals do not have any value toward the satisfying of the flesh.

Colossians 3:1:
If ye then be risen with Christ, seek those things which are above, where Christ sitteth on the right hand of God.

287

"If ye then be risen with Christ...." And we were told in Colossians 2:12 that when he arose we arose with him. Remember? "If [Since] ye then be risen with Christ, seek those things which are above, where Christ sitteth on the right hand of God." Seek the things of God; don't follow after the world's systems.

> Verse 2:
> Set your affection [*phroneō*, mind—verb] on things above, not on things on the earth.

"Mind the things above" is how the text reads. It means absolutely to do it. You set your mind on the things above. You put God's Word in your mind, and you'll see the greatness of God in Christ in you.

"Set your mind on things above, not on things on the earth," because those things which we see with our senses are temporal; but that which we see spiritually, which is God in Christ in you, is eternal.

Ladies and gentlemen, the outside world will never see the greatness of your life until they see the Christ in you. They have to read your life before they're ever going to read the Bible, I guarantee you. They have to see it live in you first. We are living epistles, known and read of

288

all men. We are to live the Word and let our lights shine before men.

> Verses 3 and 4:
> For ye are dead, and your life is hid with Christ in God.
> When Christ, *who is* our life, shall appear, then shall ye also appear with him in glory.

"When Christ, *who is* our life...." Christ is our life. That is the only thing we've got. We are dead to this world, but alive in Christ. He is right now our life. *He is our life.* And he is already seated at the right hand of the Father and he's coming back for us. That is what Colossians 3:4 is saying. "When Christ our life shall appear, then shall ye also appear with him in glory." When Christ appears, we will appear with him!

I don't know of anything more exciting and encouraging for a triumphant walk, than to live with overflowing exuberance, looking forward to appearing with Christ in glory. I don't know of any greater way to encourage God's people to live a sustained walk. Because we are rooted and built up in Christ, because we live God's Word, because we have left this world with its systems and wisdom behind, because we are the Body of Christ with each one of us having a specific

289

function, because we are completely complete in Christ Jesus—for all these reasons and more, as seen in Colossians 2 and 3, we want to walk for God as mature believers who abound in thanksgiving and thanksliving.

Oh, what a life we have, what a privilege, what a joy to serve the Lord Jesus Christ! We've been quickened together with Christ. We are completely complete in him, and we have the ability and the authority to stand with him and with one another. We look forward to the day we will appear with him in glory. That's why our hearts are comforted. That's why we are knit together in love in this extraordinary family of God.

Scripture Index

GENESIS		35:10	11
1:1	5	35:11	11
1:2	60	35:12	12
1:3	239	37	141
1:14	29	37:3	fn142
1:15	29	38	141
1:16	30	39	141
1:17	30	39:20	143
1:18	30	39:21	143
1:19	30	39:22	143
1:28	30,48	39:23	144
1:29	31	40	141
1:30	31	40:1	144
2	6	40:2	144
2:7	39	40:3	144
2:15	40	40:4	145
2:18	41	40:5	145
2:24	46,47	40:6	145
4:33	160	40:7	145
12:6,7	fn175	40:8	145
17:1	6,8,fn175	40:9	146
17:2	7	40:10	146
17:3	8	40:11	146
17:4	8	40:12	147
17:5	8,9	40:13	147
17:6	9	40:14	147
17:7	10	40:15	148
17:8	10	40:16	148
28:3	10	40:17	148
35:1-4	176	40:18	148

40:19	148	41:38	162
40:20	149	41:39	162
40:21	149	41:40	162
40:22	149	41:41	162
40:23	150	41:42	163
41	141	41:43	163
41:1	150	41:44	164
41:2	151	41:45	165
41:3	151	41:46	165
41:4	151	41:47	166
41:5	151	41:48	166
41:6	151	41:49	166
41:7	151	41:50	166
41:8	152	41:51	167
41:9	152	41:52	167
41:10	152	41:53	167
41:11	152	41:54	167
41:12	153	41:55	167
41:13	153	41:56	168
41:14	153	41:57	169
41:15	154	43:14	12
41:16	155	48	fn167
41:17	155	49:25	12
41:25	156		
41:26	156	**EXODUS**	
41:27	156	17:9	113
41:28	157	17:10	114
41:29	157	17:11	114
41:30	157	17:12	114
41:31	157	17:13	114
41:32	157	17:14	114
41:33	159	24:13	115
41:34	160	33:11	108,115
41:35	161		
41:36	161	**NUMBERS**	
41:37	161	14:6	112

14:7	112	1:2	108,110,120,121
14:8	112	1:3	123
14:9	112	1:4	125
27:18	116	1:5	125,129
27:19	116	1:6	129,134
27:20	116	1:7	130,134
27:21	116	1:8	132,136
27:22	116	1:9	134,136
27:23	116	1:10	121
32:11	113	1:11	121
32:12	113	3:6	127
		3:7	127,172
DEUTERONOMY		3:8	127
6:6	fn185	3:15	128
6:7	fn185	3:16	128
6:8	fn185	7:12	174
6:9	fn185	24:1	175
11:24	123	24:2,3	fn175
17:6	fn157	24:11	176
19:15	fn157	24:12	177
22:10	fn16	24:13	177
25:2	192	24:13,14	fn175
25:3	193	24:14	178
27	176	24:15	179,186
31:7	171	24:16	181
31:8	171	24:17	181
31:14	172	24:18	181
34:5	117	24:19	181
34:6	117	24:20	182
34:7	117	24:21	182
34:8	117	24:22	182
34:9	118	24:23	183
34:10	118	24:24	183
		24:25	183
JOSHUA		24:26	183
1:1	110,120	24:27	185

24:28	185

PSALMS
8:5	32
103:7	108
119:133	ix,206

PROVERBS
31	43

ISAIAH
40:1	279
40:2	279
41:8	9
53:6	282

JEREMIAH
13:15-17	fn187
19	190
19:14	190
19:15	190
20:1	191
20:1-6	197
20:2	192
20:3	194
20:4	195
20:5	195
20:6	196
20:7	197
20:8	197,198
20:9	197,198
21:8	200
22:9,10	fn187
48:29-32	fn187

MATTHEW
5:14	247
5:15	247
5:16	247
6:9	5
6:10	5
6:33	179
13:20	263
13:21	263
15:1-3	269
15:6	270
15:7	270
15:8	270
15:9	271,287
18:16	fn157
22:17	209
22:18	209
22:19	210
22:20	210
22:21	210

LUKE
3:12	208
3:13	208
9:57	89
9:59	89
9:60	90
9:61	90
9:62	90
10:27	50
19:1	207
19:2	208,211
19:3	212,213
19:4	213
19:5	214,215
19:6	216

19:7	217,220
19:8	217
19:9	219
19:10	220
24:27	253
24:31	254

JOHN

1	231
3:34	272
4:24	fn240
8:12	248
8:17	fn157
13:34	228

ACTS

4:12	fn221
10:9-18	fn157
16:4	266
16:5	266
22:20	fn85

ROMANS

4:5-9	61
6:23	fn234
8:24	fn62
8:25	fn62
10:9,10	278
10:17	fn222
12	100
12:1	86
12:4	95
12:5	96
12:6	96,97,98
12:7	97,98
12:8	97,98,99

13	55,93,95
13:1	55,99,101
13:2	101,102
13:3	102
13:4	103
13:5	103,104
13:6	103,104
13:7	104

I CORINTHIANS

2:14	fn24,27
3:6	266
9:1-19	fn104
9:14	fn104
12:21	285
12:27	93
12:28	93,94
14:37	226

II CORINTHIANS

4:1	242
4:2	242
4:3	243
4:4	244
4:5	245
4:6	245,246
4:7	246
6:1	16
6:14	16
6:15	17
6:16	17
6:17	17
6:18	18
11:23-27	fn237
13:1	fn157

GALATIANS

3:7	14,fn220
3:28	14
3:29	14
5	205
5:16-26	226,227
5:22	223,224
5:23	224
5:24	224
5:25	224
5:26	224
6	205
6:1	225,226,227
6:2	227,228,229,230,231
6:3	229,230
6:4	230
6:5	228,230,231
6:6	231
6:7	232,233
6:8	233,234,235
6:9	235,236
6:10	236
6:17	237

EPHESIANS

1:3	274
1:4	31,fn60
1:5	31
1:6	32
1:13	fn163
1:18	276
1:19	277
1:20	277
1:21	277
1:22	277
1:23	277

2:8	fn234
2:9	fn234
4:8	fn283
4:16	fn96
5:8	248
5:22-25	fn43
6:1-4	fn43
6:12	fn274

PHILIPPIANS

2:13	249
2:14	250
2:15	250
2:16	250
4:19	15

COLOSSIANS

2	205
2:1	255
2:2	257,284
2:3	259
2:4	259
2:5	259
2:6	262
2:7	263,264,265,267
2:8	267,268,270,271
2:9	272
2:10	273,274
2:11	275,277
2:12	276,277,288
2:13	278
2:14	279,280,282
2:15	282
2:16	283
2:17	283
2:18	283

2:19	284
2:20	286
2:21	286
2:22	286
2:23	287
3:1	287
3:2	288
3:3	289
3:4	289

I THESSALONIANS

3:2	258
3:6	260,261
3:7	262
5:5	249

II THESSALONIANS

3:10	fn41

I TIMOTHY

1:15	fn80
2:11	83
3	55,79
3:1	79,80
3:2	80,82
3:2-7	80
3:3	82
3:4	83
3:5	84
3:6	84
3:7	85
4:9	fn80
6:10	70

II TIMOTHY

1:7	241

2:11	fn80
3:16	fn225

TITUS

1	55,79
1:1	58,60,65
1:2	60,62
1:3	63
1:4	64,65
1:5	66
1:6	68,71
1:7	69,71
1:8	71
1:9	71,72
1:10	73
1:11	73
1:12	74
1:13	74,75
1:14	75
1:15	75
1:16	76
3:8	fn80

HEBREWS

4:12	200
7:25	221
11	188
11:37	188
11:38	189

JAMES

2:23	9

I PETER

3:1-8	fn43
3:7	50

I JOHN

1:5	240
1:7	241
1:9	fn248
4:20	fn229
4:21	fn229

III JOHN

2	133

REVELATION

12:9	fn232
19:11	19
19:12	19
19:13	19
19:14	19
19:15	19
19:16	20
22:5	239,240

About the Author

Victor Paul Wierwille spent several decades vigorously and prayerfully searching out the truths of God's Word. As part of his search he consulted and worked with many outstanding individuals in Christian studies for keys to power-filled, victorious living. Such men as Karl Barth, Joseph Bauer, Glenn Clark, Karl J. Ernst, Josiah Friedli, Louis C. Hessert, Elmer G. Homrighausen, E. Stanley Jones, George M. Lamsa, Richard and Reinhold Niebuhr, K.C. Pillai, Paul Tillich, Ernst Traeger, and many others were a part of Dr. Wierwille's quest to find the truths of the Word of God.

Dr. Wierwille's academic career included Bachelor of Arts and Bachelor of Theology degrees from Mission House (Lakeland) College and Seminary, graduate studies at the University of Chicago and at Princeton Theological Seminary, where he earned the Master of Theology degree in Practical Theology. Later he completed his work for the Doctor of Theology degree at Pikes Peak Bible Seminary and Burton College in Manitou Springs, Colorado.

299

For over forty years, Dr. Wierwille devoted his major energies to intensive research and teaching of the accuracy of God's Word. In 1953 he began teaching Biblical research and teaching classes on Power for Abundant Living. He was the founder and first president of The Way International, a nonsectarian, nondenominational Biblical research, teaching, and fellowship ministry. He held the presidency of The Way College of Emporia, and he was the founder and first president of several other centers of learning: The Way College of Biblical Research, Indiana Campus; Camp Gunnison—The Way Family Ranch; and LEAD Outdoor Academy International.

As Dr. Wierwille persevered in his research of the Bible, he continued to write more research works and to develop further classes in Biblical studies, including The University of Life outreach courses, an international Biblical studies correspondence school. As a dynamic lecturer, he traveled and taught worldwide, holding forth the greatness of the accuracy of God's Word with great intensity until his death in May of 1985.